Discourses of Power

'With this book, Barry Hindess sets new parameters for any future discourses on power. He unravels the confusion of power as capacity and power as right which has dogged modern political theory from Hobbes and Locke onwards, and sets out clearly the presuppositions of contemporary theories of power. On this basis, he is able to locate Foucault squarely in the mainstream of modern political thought, and to demonstrate the radicality of his attempts to refocus the analysis of power onto the nature and forms of government.

In a brief concluding chapter, Hindess sums up both the strengths and limits of Foucault's challenge to political theory, and points to the fictions of political community as constraints upon political thought which remain to be critically examined. A model of clear and effective writing, this book should be read by all students of political and social thought.'

Paul Patton, Senior Lecturer in Philosophy, University of Sydney

'Barry Hindess has crafted an elegant and incisive guide to the debates about power set in motion by Michel Foucault. He offers both a clear account of what is at stake in these debates, and a sharp critical sense of how they could develop.'

Professor R. B. J. Walker, Department of Political Science,
University of Victoria

'The combination of impeccable scholarship and original insight makes this book indispensable to all who wish to explore the complex field of modern power. Through bold and invigorating investigations of the central texts of modern political thought, Barry Hindess uncovers their conceptual anatomy and reveals the pervasive implications of flawed understandings of power from Locke to contemporary liberalism and critical theory. Through a lucid exploration of the arguments of Michel Foucault, Hindess poses us urgent and challenging questions about how one might think beyond these limited visions of political sovereignty and political community.'

Nikolas Rose, Professor of Sociology, Goldsmiths College,
University of London

for Christine

Discourses of Power:
from Hobbes to Foucault

Barry Hindess

BLACKWELL
Publishers

First published 1996
Reprinted 1996, 1997, 2001
Transferred to digital print 2004

Blackwell Publishers Ltd
108 Cowley Road
Oxford OX4 1JF, UK

Blackwell Publishers Inc
350 Main Street
Malden, Massachusetts 02148, USA

British Library Cataloguing in Publication Data
A CIP catalogue record for this book is available from the British Library

Library of Congress Cataloging in Publication Data
Hindess, Barry
Discourses of power: from Hobbes to Foucault/Barry Hindess
p. cm.
Includes bibliographical references and index.
ISBN 0–631–19092–9 — ISBN 0–631–19093–7 (pbk)
1. Power (Social sciences). I. Title.
HN49.P6H56 1995   95-8978
303.3—dc20   CIP

Typeset in Sabon 12 on 14pt
by Pure Tech Corporation, Pondicherry, India

This book is printed on acid-free paper

For the People; and truly I desire their Liberty and Freedom as much as any Body; but I must tell you that their Liberty and Freedom consists in having the Government of those Laws, by which their Life and their Goods may be most their own; 'tis not for having a share in Government [Sirs] that is nothing pertaining to 'em. A Subject and a Sovereign are clean different things. If I would have given way to an arbitrary way, for to have all Laws changed according to the Power of the Sword, I needed not to have come here; and therefore I tell you (and I pray God that it be not laid to your Charge) that I am the Martyr of the People.

Charles the First, King of England, *Speech on the Scaffold*, 1649

We need to cut off the King's head: in political theory that has still to be done.

Michel Foucault, in *Power/Knowledge*, 1980, p. 121

only that which has no history is definable

Friedrich Nietzsche, *On the Genealogy of Morals*, Essay 2, §xiii

Contents

Acknowledgements

Many people have helped in the production of this book through their encouragement, critical discussion and disagreement, or through reading and commenting on portions of the manuscript. I am particularly grateful to John Ballard, He Baogang, Mitchell Dean, Ian Hunter, Duncan Ivison, Doug McEachearn, Jeffrey Minson, Paul Patton, Philip Pettit, Nikolas Rose, Alison Smith, Rob Walker, and David West. My greatest debt, however, is to Christine Helliwell. Not only did her love and support sustain me while the book was being written (and while it was not being written) but she also made a substantial contribution to the writing itself. Without her critical and uncompromising reading, and without the work she put into its improvement, the final draft would have been considerably poorer.

1

Introduction:
Two Conceptions of Power

Two conceptions of power have dominated Western political thought in the modern period. One, which has been especially prominent in recent academic discussion, is the idea of power as a simple quantitative phenomenon. Power, in this sense, is nothing more than a kind of generalized capacity to act. The second, more complex, understanding is that of power as involving not only a capacity but also a *right* to act, with both capacity and right being seen to rest on the consent of those over whom the power is exercised. This second conception is central to much Western social and political thought although, as we shall see, its presence is often implicit rather than explicit. The aim of this book is to demonstrate the assumptions underlying both of these understandings, and the consequent implications for the manner in which questions to do with the exercise of power, and of government, are normally approached and understood within contemporary Western social and political thought. My discussion focuses particularly on the second conception, not only because its greater complexity invites more careful attention, but also because the elaboration of this conception allows us – in ways that elaboration of the first does not – to make sense of these more general questions.

Power as Simple Capacity

The first conception of power, as a simple capacity to act, is widely employed in modern Western thought. In this understanding, there is a sense in which social or political power is regarded as the same kind of thing as electrical power or the power of a motor: it is conceived as a quantitative capacity that may be put to work for a variety of purposes. People employ power in their dealings with things and in their dealings with each other. In the latter case, this conception of power implies that the wishes of those with more power will normally prevail over the wishes of those with less. It is for this reason that Weber identifies power with 'the chance of a man or a number of men to realise their own will even against the resistance of others who are participating in the action' (Weber 1978, p. 926). This conception of power as simple capacity suggests that there will be an unequal relation between those who employ power for their own purposes and those who are subject to its effects. Power, in this sense, may be used as an instrument of domination.

Many academic commentators have suggested that this is the essential meaning of power, and that what might seem to be competing understandings should properly be seen as more or less acceptable variations on this one. The implication here is that conceptions of power which cannot be reduced to this 'underlying' conception should be regarded as mistaken. Perhaps the best known statement of this position is the one set out in Lukes' *Power: a radical view* (1974). Lukes maintains there that while the concept of power is 'essentially contested' by different investigators holding different social values, the alternative 'views' of power which those values entail may nevertheless be reduced to the one underlying concept: that of power in the sense of simple quantitative capacity.

Lukes' book is an extended commentary on the debates over community power which were at the centre of American academic discussions of power in the 1960s and 1970s.[1] On one side in these debates were the elite theorists, who argued that power at both the national and the local level in America was concentrated in the hands of elites. Mills, for example, maintained that America is ruled by an elite consisting of the most influential figures in business, government and the military. Collectively they hold a 'power unequalled in human history, they have succeeded within the American system of organised irresponsibility' (Mills 1959, p. 361). Similarly, Hunter argued in his more localized study of Atlanta, Georgia, USA, that the distribution of power 'does not square with the concept of democracy we have been taught to revere' (Hunter 1953, p. 1). The elite theorists were concerned to argue not only that power is in the hands of elites, but also that the exercise of power by those elites is not responsible: that is, that they are not accountable to the people in the manner that orthodox American notions of democracy would require.

On the other side were the pluralists, led by Dahl, who argued that power in America was neither as concentrated, nor was its exercise as irresponsible, as the elite theorists maintained. The distribution of power is certainly unequal, but it does not follow that power is therefore concentrated in the hands of a unified elite. Similarly, the fact that the conduct of politics in America does not conform to standard notions of democracy need not imply that the powerful must therefore be regarded as irresponsible. Rather, it shows that these notions of democracy themselves should be modified to take into account the complexities of public life in contemporary America. Dahl's study of politics in New Haven, for example, led him to the conclusion that it 'is a republic of unequal citizens – but for all that a republic' (Dahl 1961, p. 86). While America may be a long way from the goal of political equality, Dahl maintains that it is nevertheless a society in which the people rule.

Lukes argues that these disputes reflect a conflict between two 'views' of the one underlying concept of power. The most straightforward of these, which he attributes to pluralists such as Dahl and Nelson Polsby, is the 'liberal view' that possession of power can be identified with confidence only in cases of overt conflict – since those who prevail in such cases are able to do so precisely because they do, in fact, have more power than their opponents. Lukes describes this as a 'one-dimensional view' of power. According to this 'one-dimensional' approach, it would be possible to identify a ruling elite only if there was clear evidence that the supposed elite were normally able to impose their wishes, even against majority resistance. In the absence of such evidence, the pluralists argue, the claim that America is dominated by a power elite should be regarded as mere speculation.

The other is the 'reformist' view, which Lukes attributes to anti-pluralists such as Mills and Hunter. According to this view, there are 'two faces of power', and consequently Lukes describes it as a 'two-dimensional' approach. Bachrach and Baratz (1969) maintain that the pluralist analysis focuses only on one of the two faces of power: the public face. The second, private, face of power can be seen in the covert exclusion of the interests of particular individuals or groups from consideration in legislative assemblies, council chambers and other arenas in which decisions affecting the life of the community are taken. In this way, the manifest discontent of these individuals or groups is prevented from leading to cases of overt political conflict. This view, then, suggests that approaching the study as if it involved nothing more than sorting out who prevails in any overt conflict is likely to obscure an important part of the actual exercise of power in society. In fact, according to the elite theorists, it is the *covert* uses of power which make possible the benign public representation of power as serving the general interest. On this view, it is precisely because their power enables them to manipulate the agenda of political debate that the rule of unrepresentative elites meets so little opposition in such 'democratic' communities as the United States.

Lukes has considerable sympathy for this second view of power, which he regards as much superior to the first. However, he describes this second view also as seriously incomplete. In its place he proposes a 'three-dimensional view', which he describes as 'radical in both the theoretical and political senses' (Lukes 1974, p. 9). Where the second view of power suggests that the interests of certain individuals or groups may well be excluded from political debate, Lukes goes further to argue that there may also be instances of the exercise of power in which its victims fail even to recognize that their real interests are at risk, and consequently make no attempt to defend those interests. On this view, there is a third, particularly insidious, form of power which is able to influence the thoughts and desires of its victims without their being aware of its effects.

While this 'radical' view of power had little impact on the positions adopted by the major participants in the community power debates themselves, Lukes is right to insist on its importance. This view has been most influential, perhaps, in the numerous elaborations on Karl Marx's claim that the ruling ideas are those of the ruling class. In Antonio Gramsci's discussion of bourgeois hegemony, to take just one example, the power of the bourgeoisie in advanced capitalist societies is said to be based on a combination of coercion and consent. The consent of the popular classes to bourgeois rule is possible, in Gramsci's view, only because they are not aware of their interest in the overthrow of capitalist domination. They consent, in other words, to a rule which they do not properly understand. Gramsci's argument here is not intended to deny the importance of repression and manipulation by the ruling class in advanced capitalist societies. But it does suggest that these more obvious forms of the exercise of power are not always the most effective instruments of bourgeois rule.

Lukes' account of power raises a number of problematic issues. The most important of these concern his claim that all significant contemporary usages of the term can be reduced to a single underlying concept: they are all presented as variations on the conception of power as simple capacity. Nietzsche once observed, in the course of a discussion on the concept of punishment, that 'only that which has no history is definable' (Nietzsche 1967, Essay 2, §XIII). His point here is that 'punishment' is a term which has served, and continues to serve, many different purposes, and that to propose a definition of it would inevitably be to favour some of these purposes over others. The same could be said of 'power': it would be surprising if the competing usages of such a contentious term could be circumscribed quite as neatly as Lukes' analysis suggests. What is of particular interest about claims such as Lukes', then, is not only that they are empirically questionable, as we shall see below, but also that they can be made at all.

Lukes' own discussion focuses on the community power debates of the 1960s and early 1970s, and these might seem to constitute a remarkably limited source of evidence on which to base such a wide-ranging claim. In fact, however, it would be difficult to deny that some conception of power as most essentially a matter of simple capacity has been a prominent feature of academic discussions of power since the 1950s. The most striking limitation of these discussions arises from their restricted geographical and historical concerns, since they have focused largely on conditions in the contemporary United States and other Western societies (the community power debates themselves being an excellent case in point). However, in fairness to Lukes, it should also be noted that the understanding of power as simple capacity is regularly employed in less obviously parochial contexts.

An excellent example is provided by *A History of Power from the Beginning to* AD *1760*, the first volume of Mann's *The Sources of Social Power*. Mann's discussion is instructive in different ways from that of Lukes: first, because he explicitly relates his own treatment of power to the Marxist and Weberian traditions of social theory; secondly, because his conception of power is clearly intended to encompass the whole of human history, rather than just the public life of the most affluent societies of the mid-twentieth century. After identifying power in general as 'the ability to pursue and attain goals' (Mann 1986, p. 6), Mann proceeds to define *social* power, in particular, as combining two interrelated aspects. These are, first, the power of some people over others; secondly, the power of collective action 'whereby persons in cooperation can enhance their joint power over third parties or over nature' (ibid.). Social power, then, is a matter of domination on the one hand and collective organization on the other.

This broad view of power, Mann suggests, can be derived from both the Marxist and the Weberian traditions of social theory. These traditions, he tells us, share the 'joint premise' that '*social stratification is the overall creation and distribution of power in society*. It is *the* central structure of societies because in its dual collective and distributive aspects it is the means whereby human beings achieve their goals in society' (Mann 1986, p. 10). In fact, as Mann notes, Marxists and Weberians generally go on to distinguish distinct kinds of power corresponding to each of the three fundamental spheres of social life: economic, political and cultural (the last being a matter of ideology in the one tradition and of status groupings in the other). They disagree, however, over how the relations between the powers at work in these different spheres are to be understood. Where Marxists regard economic power as most important in the final analysis, Weberians tend to argue that, in principle, there is no reason to suppose that one type of power should always predominate over any of the others. Mann's own position is clearly Weberian in this respect, although he modifies Weber by distinguishing four bases of power (economic, ideological, military and political) rather than the more usual three.

There is, of course, considerably more to Mann's discussion than the elaboration of a particular concept of power. However, what should be noted here is that within his discussion (as well as in the Marxist and Weberian traditions on which he claims to draw), the conventional distinctions between economic, political and other discrete powers in no way detract from the basic model of power as a simple quantitative phenomenon. This is because, first, each of these powers is itself conceived as a matter of simple capacity: greater economic (or ideological or military or political) power invariably prevails over less. Secondly, simply to pose the question of whether one type of power predominates over the others is itself to bring their simple quantitative character to the fore.

A similar point could be made with regard to Giddens' treatment of power within his more general theory of structuration. Power, he suggests, exhibits a particular duality of structure: on the one hand it refers to the capacity of one or more agents to 'make a difference' (Giddens 1984, p. 14), while on the other it is a structural 'property of society or the social community' (ibid., p. 15). These two aspects of power are brought together in Giddens' account by his conception of structure as not only constraining the actions of individuals, but also providing resources on which they draw in the course of interaction with others. Correlatively, action is seen as not only expressing the intentions of individual agents, but also serving to reproduce the structure in which such action takes place.

Giddens' insistence that power makes use of resources, some of which should be seen as structured properties of social systems, suggests a sense in which power can be seen as adhering to social systems, as well as to individuals and groups within them. This implies that there is more to the study of power in any society than analysis of the distribution of power amongst its members. There will always be cases in which power is used by some members of the society against the interests of others, but Giddens nevertheless insists that power 'is not intrinsically connected to the achievement of sectional interests' (ibid.). Giddens' perspective here offers a valuable corrective to the tendency of all too many discussions of power to concentrate on questions of who holds power and who does not, with the community power debates again providing a clear example. However, in spite of the advantages of his own conceptualization of power in this respect, Giddens nevertheless takes 'the most all-embracing meaning of power' (ibid.) to be a matter of capacity. It is 'the capability of the individual to "make a difference" to a pre-existing state of affairs' (ibid., p. 14). We are back, then, with Lukes' underlying concept of power: power as simple quantitative capacity. Lukes is clearly quite correct in arguing that many 'views' of power in contemporary academic discussion ultimately rest on this straightforward understanding.

Power as Legitimate Capacity

We can agree, then, that a conception of power as simple capacity is widely employed in contemporary Western societies, both by academic commentators and more generally. However, it would be a serious mistake to suggest that it underlies *all* significant contemporary usages of the term in quite the manner that Lukes' analysis would seem to require. Lukes himself appears almost to acknowledge the existence of a second major conception of power in modern Western thought when he notes that neither Arendt's nor Parsons' conceptions of power are based on this simple understanding. Unfortunately, rather than consider the implications of this fact for his claim to have identified the 'underlying concept' of power, Lukes dismisses these alternative conceptions as idiosyncratic. In particular, he argues that the treatment of power as a function of consent is 'out of line with the central meanings of "power" as traditionally understood and with the concerns that have always centrally preoccupied students of power' (Lukes 1974, p. 31).

Lukes' treatment of these alternative conceptions of power is unsatisfactory for several reasons. First, as we shall see in chapter 2, there are serious problems with the conception of power as simple capacity. If only for this reason, then, we should be wary of any attempt to dismiss alternative conceptions of power out of hand. Secondly, the conception of power as resting on consent, which Lukes treats as idiosyncratic, has in fact been at the centre of Western political and social thought throughout the modern period. Since, as was noted in the opening paragraph, the greater part of this book focuses on this more complex conception of power, I shall deal with it only briefly at this point.

The place to start, as Lukes does, is with Arendt's and

Parsons' treatments of power. While Arendt's and Parsons' analyses are by no means equivalent, they do share a view of power as fundamentally dependent on the consent of those over whom it is exercised. Parsons, for example, defines power as:

> the generalised capacity to secure the performance of binding obligations by units in a system of collective action when the obligations are legitimised with reference to their bearing on collective goals and where in the case of recalcitrance there is a presumption of enforcement by negative situational sanctions. (Parsons 1969a, p. 361; quoted in Lukes 1974, pp. 27–8)

Parsons is not renowned for the felicity of his prose, but this definition encapsulates the fundamental idea of power as a capacity that operates primarily on the basis of its legitimacy, and therefore by means that presume the consent of those over whom it is exercised.

There is an obvious sense in which the idea of a power that operates on the basis of consent can be seen as invoking the more general notion of power as quantitative capacity. Nevertheless, as we shall see in chapter 2, the presumption that consent is the key to its exercise conflicts with Lukes' account of the 'underlying conception' of power in a number of crucial respects. The more important point to be noted here, however, is that since capacity and legitimacy are intimately related in the conception of power as a function of consent, its employment in any particular context invariably raises questions of both fact and evaluation. Its conflation of fact and value is one of the reasons why this conception appears to have fallen out of favour with many social scientists since the Second World War. However, we shall see that disagreements amongst those who claim to see the conception of power as relating primarily to simple quantitative capacity frequently revolve around broader concerns with the political constitution of society and with the proper relations between rulers and ruled: that is, with questions of value concerning the relationship between power and consent. In fact, much of the diversity of contemporary interpretations of power – and much of the confusion arising from this diversity – reflects the vicissitudes of the slippery idea of a power that rules through the consent of the governed. While Lukes associates each of the three 'views' of power which he identifies with its own distinctive set of social values (the one-dimensional view with liberalism, the two-dimensional view with reformism, the three-dimensional view with radicalism), the conception of power as resting on consent has, in fact, been employed across a considerable variety of political and intellectual standpoints. Indeed, we shall see in chapter 4 that Lukes' own radical 'view' of power makes considerable use of precisely this conception. A central claim of this book, then, is that far from being idiosyncratic, the treatment of power as resting on consent has played a central part in Western political thought throughout the modern period.

The importance of this understanding of power is particularly clear in the case of discussions of sovereign power; that is, in discussions of the power that is thought to be exercised by the ruler of a state or by its (central) government. This is now usually conceived of as a political power that is subordinated to no superior and, more importantly for our purposes, as dependent on the implicit consent of its subjects and therefore on the rights and obligations which that consent entails.[2] The sovereign (or government) is conceived of as issuing commands which the subjects – by virtue of the consent which they are presumed to have given to the sovereign's rule – are expected to treat as having the character of binding obligations. While the consent of its subjects, then, is thought to provide the sovereign with the *right* to govern, the attendant obligations on those subjects are supposed to provide the sovereign with the *capacity* to do so. This idea of a power involving some such combination of both right and capacity is commonly employed in the discussion of government. But it can also be used in other contexts where agreement between the parties concerned is thought to establish a pattern of rights and obligations – the contract of employment and the contract of marriage providing two very different contemporary examples.

The basis of the subjects' obedience may be conceptualized in a number of ways. Ullman (1965, 1966) maintains that in the European Middle Ages obedience was thought to follow from the recognition that all power comes from God: in obeying their temporal or spiritual rulers, the subjects were obeying God. On this view, we are all born subjects. In contrast, the characteristically modern view, which is the focus of my argument in this book, is that we are born free[3] – although we might in fact find ourselves in chains. The status of individuals as subject to the legitimate power of their sovereign, and the obligations on both sides which that status is thought to entail, are here conceived of as resulting from explicit or implicit contracts of the kinds considered in chapters 2 and 3 below. While the idea of a community in which legitimate power rests on the consent of its members finds its most forceful expression in the various forms of contract theory, it also plays a major role in many influential styles of political discussion. We shall see in chapter 4, for example, that it provides both Lukes' 'radical' view of power and contemporary critical theory with a normative ideal against which the pernicious effects of non-legitimate powers can be measured.

Structure of the Book

In developing the points and themes set out above, I have made considerable use, in the first instance, of Hobbes' *Leviathan* (published 1651) and of Locke's *Second Treatise on Government* and his *Essay Concerning Human Understanding* (both published in 1689). The attention devoted to Hobbes and Locke is not intended to suggest that they are the only, or even the most important, figures in the modern development of political thought. Rather, I make use of them in order to isolate certain issues for discussion and clarification. On the one hand, Hobbes and Locke give clear and forceful expression to themes that continue to inform contemporary debates about political power and government. On the other hand, their work is sufficiently remote to allow those themes to be examined while maintaining a certain distance from their contemporary manifestations.

After this short introduction, chapter 2 begins the discussion of these broader concerns with an examination of Hobbes' account of sovereign power. Starting from a formal definition in *Leviathan* chapter X of the 'power of a man' as 'his present means to obtain some future apparent Good' (Hobbes 1968, p. 150), Hobbes goes on to describe sovereign power as combining the powers of many individuals. This description is significant for two reasons. First, it suggests that diverse particular powers can be combined to form a power greater than any one of them. In this respect, Hobbes' notion of sovereign power can be regarded as an early elaboration of the conception of power as simple quantitative capacity. The first part of chapter 2 uses the community power debates to illustrate the contemporary significance of this conception of power, and proceeds to explore some of its limitations. The most important of these concern the implication that the outcomes of conflict are invariably determined by the 'quantities' of power available to the contending parties. I argue that this is, at best, a gross oversimplification, useful enough perhaps for polemical purposes, but of limited analytical utility – in spite of the efforts of far too many social scientists to make it work.

Secondly, Hobbes' description is significant because it implies that the power of the sovereign really is a *power* in the sense given in his formal definition. It is a power that is greater than the power of any single subject or group of subjects, since it combines the powers of all of them. However, Hobbes' account of how that sovereign power is constituted in presumed acts of authorization by numerous individual subjects presents a rather different picture. This suggests that sovereign power is a *right* to make use of the powers of its subjects, but it does not follow from this, as Hobbes would sometimes have us believe, that the sovereign will therefore have an effective *capacity* to make use of those powers. Hobbes' argument here involves a confusion between the idea of power as a capacity and the idea of power as a right: a confusion that is endemic to modern political theory.

For all its problems, the treatment of the sovereign as the single most important power in a society, and as a power that works primarily by means of decisions which its subjects normally accept as binding, has dominated much of the discussion of power in the modern period. I close the chapter by noting how these assumptions surface in contemporary discussions of democracy and in the community power debates.

Chapter 3 takes up another aspect of the problematic idea of sovereign power. Locke's *Second Treatise on Government* begins by defining political (that is, sovereign) power as a *right* to make laws and enforce them, and to defend the commonwealth from injury. However, it goes on to consider the concepts of usurpation and tyranny, according to which political power may be exercised in the absence of its constitutive right. Here, too, we see a confusion between power as capacity and power as right.

What is at issue in the concepts of usurpation and tyranny is the question of the *legitimacy* of power, which Locke analyses in terms of the rational consent of the governed. This account of legitimacy implies that other kinds of power may be required to deal with those who are unable to give their rational consent to government, because they do not possess (or are treated as if they do not possess) the necessary legal or intellectual capacities. In this respect, the idea of a government that operates by consent is entirely capable of being used to provide a rationale for its contrary: that is, for a paternalistic power that is not intended to be accountable to those who are subjected to its effects, since they are regarded as capable neither of granting, nor of withholding, their rational consent to its exercise. On the other hand, this same conception of legitimate government also provides the foundation for a radical critique of political power – an aspect which was taken up in the colonies of North America and the absolutist regimes of eighteenth-century Europe, and which later emerged as a major theme of the American community power debates.

Locke's *Second Treatise* poses the question of the legitimacy or otherwise of political power in terms of an ideal model of a political community governed by civil law; that is, by a system of laws laid down and maintained by a power which is itself sustained by the rational consent of the governed. Book II of his *Essay Concerning Human Understanding* insists that two other kinds of law also play an important part in the government of human behaviour. These are the divine law and 'the Law of Opinion or Reputation'. Locke argues that our moral understandings are formed as a result of the rewards and sanctions occasioned by our conformity or non-conformity to law. He suggests that the third law, the law of opinion, has governed the greater part of human behaviour throughout history. It works through people expressing their approval and disapproval 'of the actions of those whom they live amongst, and converse with' (*Essay*, Book II, ch. XXVIII, para. 10; 1957, pp. 353–4). This is a law that relies on no central authority, for either its enunciation or its enforcement. It is generated and sustained by the social interaction that takes place within the daily life of what later writers would call 'civil society' or the 'public sphere'.[4] The idea of a law – and especially of a morality – that arises out of the life of society itself has provided a significant motivation for political action in modern European history, most spectacularly, of course, in the French and subsequent revolutions.

While it might seem to lead my discussion away from the concept of power, this Lockean account of morality is important here for two reasons. One relates to Foucault's focus on how the effects of power (and of governmental power in particular) are produced: that is, on the techniques and the rationalities of power. In this respect, the significance of Locke's discussion of morality is that it furnishes the rationale for a variety of governmental devices intended to reform the behaviour of those whose habits of thought and of behaviour are regarded as undesirable. Locke himself sketches a number of such devices in his writings on education and in his brutal proposals for reform of the Poor Law administration. Ideas that in one context could be seen as laying the foundations for a moral critique of political power could also, in another context, be seen as justifying the exercise of governmental powers designed to improve the quality of its subjects.

Locke's treatment of morality is important, secondly, because it describes a dispersed form of social regulation that not only acts directly on the behaviour of its subjects but also moulds their thoughts and desires. I argue in the final section of chapter 4 that the idea of such a pervasive and insidious control represents the core of Lukes' third dimension of power, a conception that relates to the Gramscian notion of hegemony and to a central part of the analysis of power in contemporary critical theory.

In effect, Locke offers influential accounts of two rather different models of the human person, both of which have played an important part in Western political thought. One is the robust model of an autonomous rational individual whose consent, or lack of consent, determines the legitimacy or otherwise of political power. The other is that of a considerably more plastic individual, whose habits of thought, and therefore standards of judgement, are formed in the course of everyday interaction within what would now be called civil society. Contemporary critical theory combines this second view of the person with a broadly Marxist understanding of civil society as an arena of class conflict. On this account, the morality that arises out of the life of civil society reflects the state of relations between the classes. The person, whose thoughts and desires are moulded in the daily life of civil society, thus may well be the unsuspecting victim of an insidious form of class power. This idea underlies much of critical theory's analysis of modern society, and it provides the model for Lukes' 'radical' view of power.

Finally, no account of the vicissitudes of the idea of sovereign power can afford to ignore Foucault's repeated claim that established ways of thinking about power are profoundly unsatisfactory. At the most general level, Foucault conceives of power in terms of attempts to influence the actions of those who are free; that is, of those whose behaviour is not wholly determined by physical constraints. This simple point appears to have a number of striking consequences for the analysis of power, the most obvious being that it undermines any understanding of it in merely quantitative terms. These are discussed in the first part of chapter 5.

I have already suggested that an important part of what is at issue in the diversity of conceptions of power relates to broader concerns with the political constitution of society and with the proper relations between ruler and ruled. To suggest that traditional conceptions of power are unsatisfactory is also to suggest that those broader concerns might themselves be misconceived. Chapter 5 therefore goes on to examine Foucault's treatment of power with particular reference to his account of *government* as that has emerged in the societies of the modern West. In fact, Foucault's understanding of power appears to have changed shortly after the completion of his studies of the disciplines (1979a) and the first volume of *The History of Sexuality* (1979b). Where his earlier discussions of power make no clear distinction between power and domination, his later discussions offer a more complex view in which governmental technologies are located 'between the games of power and the states of domination' (Foucault 1988, p. 19). Foucault's most extended treatments of government belong to this second period. Accordingly, it is his later, more complex, understanding of power that is the primary focus of my discussion.

Standard contemporary accounts of government have tended to focus on what Foucault calls the 'city–citizen' model, in which subjects are regarded as citizens, and governments are seen to rule by their rational consent. Foucault regards this model as unsatisfactory on several counts, not least of which is its confusion (as noted above) of power as capacity with power as right. But of greater significance for my discussion here are two further points. One concerns Foucault's objection that the

city–citizen model provides a relatively undifferentiated
account of relations between ruler and ruled – at least in
so far as the ruled are also regarded as citizens. The other
is that the model of rule on the basis of consent offers an
account of the *legitimacy* of power, while Foucault is
more concerned to understand the means whereby the
effects of power are produced. His interest, in other
words, is in the techniques and the rationalities of power,
and of governmental power in particular. From this perspective, Foucault locates the government of the state
within a broader framework which also embraces the
government of oneself and of a household.

Foucault regards government in its most general sense
as a modality of the exercise of power which is concerned
with the conduct of conduct – and, in the case of a
household or a community, with conducting the conduct
of others. Unfortunately, while Foucault examined at
length questions to do with the government of others in
lectures at the Collège de France in 1978 and 1979, much
of his work on this issue remains unpublished. Partly for
this reason, his analysis of government has received less
critical attention than other aspects of his treatment of
power.[5] Since this broader understanding of government
will therefore be unfamiliar to many readers, much of
chapter 5 is devoted to outlining the main features of
Foucault's account. In addition to his general understanding of government, this chapter also examines Foucault's treatments of the specific rationalities of
government associated with discipline, the 'shepherd–
flock' model and liberalism. The first two present models
of relations between ruler and ruled that are considerably
more intimate, differentiated and continuous than the
city–citizen model would suggest. As for liberalism, this
is usually regarded as a normative political doctrine concerned with the defence of individual liberty against the
state. We shall see that Foucault's account of liberalism

as a specific rationality of government marks a significant departure from the standard usage. However, the point to be noted here is that Foucault presents all three rationalities as operating at a number of levels, ranging from external supervision and regimentation to the inculcation of techniques of self-regulation and personality modification. One significant result of his treatment of personality attributes as effected by the work of government is to undermine the perception of the person as autonomous moral agent which plays such an important part in the model of government as based on rational consent. The concept of sovereign power may be central to the political discourse of the modern West but, at least in Foucault's view, it also provides a seriously incomplete account of the political rationality of modern government.

The final chapter assesses how radical Foucault's alternative is. I explore this issue by considering, first, the significance of his critique of political theory, and, secondly, the parallels and differences between Foucault's arguments and those of critical theory. I argue that Foucault is largely successful in escaping from the presuppositions, and the problems, of the conception of power as a function of consent, and in particular, that much of his analysis precludes any utopian conception of human emancipation of the kind proposed by critical theory. Nevertheless, there are elements in his treatment of domination that serve to resurrect many of critical theory's traditional concerns. I conclude by qualifying Foucault's claim that political theory is 'obsessed with the person of the sovereign' (Foucault 1980, p. 121). Political theory certainly does have its obsessions, and many of these are indeed concerned with relations between sovereigns and subjects. However, as the argument of the preceding chapters will have shown, it is not so much the *person* of the sovereign that is at issue here. On the contrary, the principal obsession of modern political theory is with the idea of a community of autonomous persons whose consent provides their sovereign (or their government) with both the right and the capacity to rule. The idea of such a community is widely (and somewhat ambiguously) employed, both in a more or less descriptive sense and as a normative point of reference, not only in academic political analysis but also more generally in political life. In either case, of course, it is commonly – and correctly – regarded as something of a fiction. We should not be surprised, then, to find that the modern Western ideal of a political community consisting of autonomous persons is such a fertile source of both confusion and dispute.

2

'that Mortal God': Hobbes on Power and the Sovereign

Chapter X of Hobbes' *Leviathan* opens with a deceptively simple definition of power: 'The power of a man is his present means to obtain some future apparent Good. And it is either Originall, or Instrumentall' (ch. X; 1968 p. 150).[1] The first of these (also called Naturall) refers to faculties of body or mind such as 'extraordinary Strength, Forms, Prudence, Arts, Eloquence, Liberality, Nobility' (ibid.). The second refers to 'those powers, which acquired by these, or by fortune, are means and instruments to acquire more: as Riches, Reputation, Friends, and the secret working of God, which men call Good Luck' (ibid.).

Power in this view, then, refers to any one, or to any combination, of a remarkably heterogeneous set of attributes which appear to have in common the fact that they may be useful to their possessor in pursuit of at least some of his or her purposes. It is this same understanding of power that informs Mann's claim that in 'its most general sense, power is the ability to pursue and attain goals through mastery of one's environment' (Mann 1986, p. 6). Similarly, Giddens insists that action

depends upon the capability of the individual to 'make a difference' to a pre-existing state of affairs

or course of events. An agent ceases to be such if he
or she loses the capability to 'make a difference', that
is, to exercise some sort of power. (Giddens 1984, p.
14)

Power, in other words, is a condition of human agency.

If this view of power were to be interpreted in its most
straightforward sense, then there would be little that
could usefully be said about power in general. Power
refers to a heterogeneous collection of attributes and possessions that need have little in common – except for the
fact that they might be useful in the pursuit of some
human purpose or other. Rather than investigate the
properties of power as such, any serious inquiry would
have to concern itself separately with the discrete powers
associated with extraordinary Strength or Eloquence, or
with Riches, the secret working of God and other such
attributes, as well as with the diverse uses to which those
powers can be put. However, most of those who choose
to write about power have been reluctant to follow the
self-denying ordinance which such an interpretation
would seem to require. In its place we find a second
interpretation: one in which power refers not to extraordinary Strength, Eloquence, Riches or whatever, but
rather to something that these various attributes are
thought to have in common.

As we shall see in connection with his account of
sovereign power, Hobbes in fact goes on to write as if the
discrete powers of many individuals could be 'united by
consent' (*Leviathan* ch. X; 1968 p. 150) to form a power
greater than any of them. In another context he tells us
that 'because the power of one man resisteth and hin-
dereth the effects of the power of another: power is
simply no more, but the excess of the power of one above
that of another' (Hobbes 1928, p. 26). In these comments, Hobbes presents a view of power that departs

from the simplicity of his initial definition in a number of important respects. First, it suggests that power should really be seen as a quantitative and cumulative phenomenon. Power, in other words, is not to be confused with qualities that are particular to certain attributes. Rather it is to be understood as some common stuff, some shared underlying capacity or essence of effectiveness, which each of those attributes possesses in some quantity, and which accounts for their utility in obtaining 'future apparent Goods'. In similar vein Giddens refers to 'transformative capacity' as being 'the most all-embracing meaning of power' (Giddens 1984, p. 15). Agents draw upon and make use of various resources in the course of their actions but, Giddens insists, 'power itself is not a resource. Resources are media through which power is exercised . . .' (ibid., p. 16). Power, in other words, is not to be confused with the means through which it is exercised in any particular case: rather, power as transformative capacity is what diverse resources have in common. Here too, power is presented as if it were a generalized essence of effectiveness.

There is also a second respect in which Hobbes writes of power as if it were capable of aggregation. Not only do the powers of different persons represent quantities of a common underlying capacity, they can also be combined to form a power greater than any one of them. 'The Greatest of humane Powers', he tells us, 'is that which is compounded of the Powers of most men, united by consent, in one person . . . that has the use of all their powers' (*Leviathan* ch. X; 1968, p. 150). What is at stake here, of course, is the collective power noted in chapter 1 'whereby persons in cooperation can enhance their joint power over third parties or over nature' (Mann 1986, p. 6). In fact, Hobbes appears to suggest that these powers can be united by the *consent* of the individuals concerned – but this is to ignore the organization required to achieve the effective coordination of the actions of numerous independent persons. I return to the consequences of Hobbes' neglect in the following section.

Finally, the understanding of power as quantitative capacity involves a sense of determinism that is not required by the view of power as the ability of an individual, as Giddens puts it, to 'make a difference' (Giddens 1984, p. 14). If to have power is always to possess the essence of effectiveness in some definite quantity, then those who possess a greater quantity of that essence obviously will be more effective than those with a lesser quantity. Where there are differences over what 'future apparent Goods' should be pursued and over who should receive them, the desires of those with more power are likely to prevail over the desires of those who have less. In place of a view of power as the ability to make a difference we now have the view of power as a quantitative capacity to secure one's own preferred outcome.

This view of power as a quantitative and mechanical phenomenon which determines the capacity of actors to realize their will or to secure their interests has been enormously influential in the modern period. Any undergraduate student of politics or of sociology since the 1970s, for instance, would be familiar with Weber's definition of power as 'the chance of a man or a number of men to realise their own will even against the resistance of others who are participating in the action' (Weber 1978, p. 926). Most will have been exposed to the American community power debates of the 1950s, either directly or through the portrayal of those debates in Lukes' hugely successful *Power: a radical view* (1974). I have already sketched the outline of those debates in chapter 1; here I simply wish to stress (as Lukes himself has done) that in spite of their many differences, both sides in this debate operated according to a quantitative conception of power. On the one side, for instance, Mills writes: 'By the powerful we mean, of course, those who are able to realise their will even if others resist it' (Mills 1959, p. 9). On the other side, Dahl insists that 'A has power over B to the extent that he can get B to do something that B would not otherwise do' (Dahl 1957, p. 204).

The great attraction of this conception of power as quantitative capacity for so many social scientists is that it appears to promise an easy means of identifying who has power and who has not. If power may be quantified, then the investigation of the distribution and the uses of power in society becomes a straightforward empirical matter. At the simplest level some have claimed that the location of those who are 'powerful' involves little more than identification of those in possession of attributes and possessions of the kind that appear in Hobbes' lists. This is in fact the basis of the 'reputational' method for the identification of powerful individuals employed by Hunter in *Community Power Structure* (1953).

In *The Power Elite*, Mills uses institutional location as the primary indicator of the possession of power:

No one can be truly powerful unless he has access to the command of major institutions, for it is over these institutional means of power that the truly powerful are, in the first instance, powerful. Higher politicians and key officials of government command such institutional power; so do admirals and generals, and so do the major owners and executives of the larger corporations. Not all power, it is true, is anchored in and exercised by means of such institutions, but only within and through them can power be more or less continuous and important. (Mills 1959, p. 9)

Here too, possession of the appropriate attribute is regarded as *prima facie* evidence of the possession of power.

Critics of Hunter and Mills were quick to point out that appearances may be misleading, and that it might therefore be a mistake to identify as powerful those who appear to possess such attributes: behind the top executive or the figure with the attribute of Reputation there may be other, less public powers pulling the strings. They argued that the powerful should be identified not by focusing on such attributes and other representations of power, but rather by concentrating directly on the effects of the quantitative essence of power. Dahl, for instance, tells us that to see where power really lies in such cases we must look for evidence of its effects – which is to say, that in the first instance we should investigate who prevails in the event of disagreement:

> I do not see how anyone can suppose that he has established the dominance of a specific group in a community or a nation without basing his analysis on the careful examination of a series of concrete decisions. And these decisions must either constitute the universe or a fair sample of the universe of key political decisions taken in the political system. (Dahl 1958, p. 286)

I will return to the significance of Dahl's second sentence towards the end of this chapter. What should be noted here is that both Hunter and Mills on the one side and their pluralist critics on the other appear to regard the distribution of power as a matter for empirical inquiry.

Yet in spite of increasing methodological sophistication, the promise of this conception of power as quantitative capacity in this respect has not been realized. One reason for this is that such a conception is itself profoundly flawed. First, there is the heterogeneity of the bases of power noted above – that is, of the attributes and means of action at the disposal of individuals. No doubt there are attributes and resources that can be deployed in a wide variety of situations and in the pursuit of many kinds of objectives – intelligence and money are familiar examples. But it would be foolish to pretend that all resources at the disposal of individuals or groups could be so flexible. Imagine a contest involving the power of extraordinary Strength on the one side and the power of Riches on the other, or an international dispute in which tanks are pitted against submarines. There is little point in considering these cases in terms of the sheer quantities of power involved on the two sides. What matters rather is the presence or the absence of conditions under which the means of action available to the contending parties can in fact be deployed. Extraordinary Strength may well prevail under some conditions, but under other conditions Riches can simply buy whatever is required for Strength to be put down.

The notion of power as capacity to secure one's preferred outcome obscures the effects of the particular attributes and means of action available to individuals or groups. Means of action of different kinds will be effective under different conditions, and in this respect the idea of an underlying common substance or essence of power is clearly unsatisfactory. Dahl (1957) introduces the idea of the *scope* of power to get around this problem. He tells us that rather than assume a universally effective form of power, we should consider powers of a more limited kind, which can be deployed in relation to some outcomes but not others. Similarly, as I noted in chapter 1, many other theorists conventionally distinguish between political, economic and other powers that operate in different areas of social life. Or again, Wrong maintains that many stable social relations may be characterized by a certain balance of power and a division of scopes between the parties concerned.

Thus a wife may rule in the kitchen, while her husband controls the disposition of the family income. Or a labor union, as in the unions of seamen and longshoremen, controls the hiring, while the employer dictates the time and place of work. (Wrong 1979, pp. 10–11)

Both of Wrong's examples will now seem somewhat dated, and we shall see in a moment that they suggest a further difficulty with the understanding of power as quantitative capacity. What should be noted here is that while the contextual aspect of the exercise of power is emphasized in these elaborations, this by no means detracts from the central model of power as a quantitative phenomenon. Such distinct and contextualized powers come into conflict only if there is some degree of overlap between their respective scopes; for example, where what transpires in the wife's domain is itself affected by the husband's disposition of the family income. Where they do come into conflict it is still the quantitative character of power that is paramount: more power will invariably prevail over less. If we only had perfect information, then it would seem that the outcome of any conflict could be predicted by adding up the resources available to each side and subtracting one total from the other. Indeed, it is precisely for this reason that, in the absence of perfect information, Dahl proposes to treat the study of who in fact prevails in the event of conflict as providing the best possible evidence of the distribution of power.

The implication that once the power available to contending parties is known, the outcome of any conflict between them should thus be entirely predictable, brings us to the second problem with the conception of power as quantitative capacity. There are certainly cases in which the imbalance of resources so favours one side in a dispute that the outcome can scarcely be in doubt.

However, to treat such cases as paradigmatic for the analysis of what happens in *all* cases of conflicting interests or objectives is misleading in two important respects.[2] First, the resources available to the parties engaged in a dispute will normally depend on conditions that are not entirely within the control of the contending parties themselves. I have already referred to Dahl's argument that many kinds of power have definite and delimited scopes: they can be deployed in some contexts but not in others, and only in pursuit of a certain range of objectives. To say that power has a definite and delimited scope is also to say that its utility depends on conditions that are not themselves within the control of those who possess that power. Many of the powers available to unions and employers, to take one of Wrong's examples, will depend on their relationships with police and with a variety of other more or less corrupt government agencies – and also, of course, on the legislation which those agencies are expected to implement. Such relationships may change, as may the relevant legislation – and they will often change for reasons that have little to do with the actions of the unions and employers concerned. This means that the powers of contending parties, and the scopes of those powers, cannot always be envisaged in terms of the fixed quantities that the mechanical model requires.[3]

In fact, Wrong's example also serves to illustrate a similar point with regard to powers that are a matter of organization, namely, that the extent and utility of such powers will depend on conditions that are only partly determined by the organization concerned. In their efforts to coordinate the actions of their members and employees, both unions and employers make use of their legal rights – and sometimes therefore of law-enforcement agencies – and they also make use of a variety of control techniques operating through the collection of information, hierarchical chains of command, and so on. The effectiveness of such devices will depend on relationships with other organizations of the kind noted above, and on the market situations of employers and employees. Finally, all attempts at coordination will be subject to obstacles of various kinds, ranging from more or less organized resistance to disorganized bloody-mindedness or indifference. These points too suggest that the powers of organization can hardly be seen as given quantities in the manner required by the quantitative understanding of power.

The second and more important respect in which the conception of power as quantitative capacity is misleading follows directly from its presumption that *quantities* of power should be seen as being decisive. This presumption means that the model can take no account of how tactics employed in the course of the conflict may affect its outcome, either directly or through their effects on the behaviour of third parties. Even if the issues noted above could be discounted, it should still be clear that the possession of power with a suitable scope does not guarantee that such power will always be employed to the best effect, or even that it will be employed at all. The advantage of extraordinary Strength may count for little if its possessor is distracted or drunk when the action takes place.

The fundamental problem with the conception of power as quantitative capacity lies in its inability to allow for the indeterminacy of conflict. In effect, it treats the outcome of conflict not as something produced in the course of conflict itself, but rather as the simple product of initial conditions – as if all cases of conflict were really just the working out of their own pre-ordained scripts. Once the exercise of power is seen as involving the use of definite resources under conditions that are not entirely determined by the persons concerned, then it ceases to be

a capacity to secure one's preferred objectives. I⟨
and at best, it becomes a capacity to act in pu⟨
those objectives.

In view of its glaring deficiencies the most interesting
question raised by the quantitative conception of power
is why it is that so many students of power have been
able to take it seriously. This question brings us to a
further reason for the failure of that conception of power
to live up to its investigative promise, viz. (as I have
already suggested) that most debates about power in the
modern period have been animated by broader concerns
that are frequently obscured in methodological discussions of the kind that have dominated the community
power debates themselves. These concerns relate to the
effects of the idea of sovereignty for the understanding
of the political constitution of society, and to questions
about the legitimacy of power and about the relations
between power and subjectivity.

Many of these broader concerns are addressed in Parsons' influential critique of what he calls the 'zero-sum'
conception of power. 'Zero-sum' is a technical term
taken from the theory of games initially developed by
von Neumann and Morgenstern (1944). It refers to a
property of those competitive games in which a fixed
quantity of assets are at stake – so that the various
possible outcomes of the game can be seen as redistribut-
ing those assets amongst the players. With regard to
power, the 'zero-sum' approach suggests that, since there
is only so much of the stuff to go round, any gain in the
power of one individual or group must involve a corresponding loss of power on the part of others. From this
perspective, the most important questions to ask in any
investigation of power are to do with its distribution,
that is: who has power and who has not?

Parsons' argument is not that questions of distribution
are illegitimate, but rather that the zero-sum approach

directs attention away from other important questions to
do with how power itself is produced and the social conditions on which its existence depends. Parsons draws a
forceful analogy here between power and wealth: questions of the distribution of wealth are not unimportant,
but they should not be confused with questions of the
production and reproduction of that wealth. If power is to
be seen as something that is produced in, and is dependent
on, definite social conditions then its effectiveness must
also be analysed as a function of the particularities of
those conditions. This requires a conception of power as
something more substantial than would be allowed by the
idea of a generalized essence of effectiveness underlying
various diverse attributes and means of action.

Parsons' own definition of power was cited in chapter
1. Power, he tells us, is:

> the generalised capacity to secure the performance of
> binding obligations by units in a system of collective
> action when the obligations are legitimised with refer-
> ence to their bearing on collective goals and where in
> the case of recalcitrance there is a presumption of
> enforcement by negative situational sanctions. (Par-
> sons 1969a, p. 361)

Parsons' 'power' is a capacity that is generalized in the
sense that it may be used for numerous diverse purposes,
but it is also a function of very particular conditions.
This particularity allows Parsons to distinguish power
from force, persuasion and other means that may be used
in the attempt to get others to conform to some desired
course of action. It also allows him to show why the
amount of power in a society should not be seen as a
fixed quantity. The power available to a society at any
given time will depend on the capacity of that society to
generate and to sustain amongst its members the belief

that the actions of those in positions of authority are indeed legitimate. The analogy here is between money and power: just as loss of confidence in the one case leads to an increasing resort to barter, so a loss of consent in the other leads to an increasing resort to coercion.

Much of what Parsons has to say about power depends, of course, on his more general sociological functionalism. However, the key to his understanding of power lies in the idea that the *consent* of its subjects provides an authority with the *capacity* to make use of their actions. The most influential version of that idea is the modern Western notion of sovereignty, and in this respect Parsons' treatment of power shares many of the strengths and many of the weaknesses of a long tradition of political thought. This point brings us back to Hobbes' discussion of power.

The Power of a Commonwealth

While it may be tempting to regard this conception of power as simple capacity as Hobbes' central contribution to the analysis of power, it would be a mistake to do so. In fact, the greater part of his political argument makes use of a different, and far more complex, view of power.

> The Greatest of humane Powers, is that which is compounded of the Powers of most men, united by consent, in one person, Naturall, or Civill, that has the use of all their Powers, depending on his will; such is the Power of a Common-wealth: Or depending on the wills of each particular; such as is the Power of a Faction, or of diverse factions leagued. Therefore to have Servants, is Power; To have friends, is Power: for they are strengths united. (*Leviathan*, ch. X; 1968, p. 150)

In Hobbes' account, this power of a single commanding will is constituted by a multiplicity of individual acts
of authorization, in which each subordinate person
agrees to make another the author of his actions. In such
cases we must distinguish between the person of the actor
and that of the author, i.e. 'he that owneth his words and
actions' (ibid., ch. XVI; 1968, p. 218):

> For that which in speaking of goods and possessions,
> is called an Owner . . .; speaking of Actions is called
> Author. And as the Right of possession, is called
> Dominion; so the right of doing any action is called
> Authority'. (ibid.)

To make another the author of one's actions is to assign
to that person all the relevant rights and responsibilities.
    The most important instance of this kind of power is
the power of a commonwealth, which Hobbes describes
as a power constituted by Covenant:

> as if every man should say to every man, I Authorise
> and give up my Right of Governing my selfe, to this
> Man, or to this Assembly of men, on this condition,
> that thou give up thy Right to him, and Authorise all
> his Actions in like manner. (ibid., ch. XVII; 1968, p.
> 227)

Why should people enter into such a Covenant? The
risk of invasion from outside is one reason, but Hobbes
also writes of another. All humankind, it seems, is possessed by 'a perpetual and restless desire of Power after
power, that ceaseth onely in Death' (ibid., ch. XI; 1968,
p. 161). This is not so much because every individual is
driven by an insatiable greed for power. Rather, it is a
matter of elementary prudence: a person 'cannot assure
the power and means to live well, which he hath present,

without the acquisition of more' (ibid.). Hobbes therefore maintains that the only way to prevent a perpetual war of all against all is for people to erect a common power, greater than any of them. The fundamental purpose of the Covenant, then, is the preservation of peace and security.

The Common-wealth created through such multiple acts of Covenant is invested in a single person: i.e., Leviathan. 'And he that carryeth this Person, is called Soveraigne' (ibid., ch. XVII; 1968, p. 228). The 'sovereign power' wielded by this person is constituted in 'the strength and means' (ibid.) of all his subjects; his subjects are the authors of the power of their sovereign. Through the Covenant the sovereign is authorized to use such power as he thinks best, in order to ensure the 'Peace and Common Defence' (ibid.) of his subjects.

It makes no difference to Hobbes' argument whether the sovereign obtains its power by voluntary agreement of its subjects or by force. In both cases the motivation for the Covenant is the same: fear. The difference between the two is simply:

> That men who choose their Sovereign, do it for fear
> of one another, and not of him whom they Institute:
> But in [the other] case, they subject themselves to
> him they are afraid of. (ibid., ch. XX; 1968, p. 252)

Hobbes regards sovereignty, then, as established by the act of authorization itself, regardless of the motivation lying behind that act.

Although Hobbes presents his account of sovereign power as if it were a straightforward extension of his treatment of power in general, this is obviously misleading: the notion of 'sovereign power' simply does not work in terms of the conception of power as simple capacity already outlined. The most striking difficulty in this respect concerns the assumption that diverse individual powers may be neatly aggregated to produce a power of overwhelming proportions, whose 'present means to obtain some future apparent Good' is equal to the sum total of all its constituent parts:

> For by this Authoritie, given him by every particular man in the Common-wealth, he [Leviathan] hath the use of so much Power and Strength conferred on him, that by terror thereof, he is inabled to forme the wills of them all, to Peace at home, and mutual ayd against their enemies abroad. (*Leviathan*, ch. XVII; 1968, p. 227–8)

An obvious problem here concerns the heterogeneity of powers noted above. It is far from clear that the eloquence of one person, the strength of a second, and the reputation of a third, can be added together to form a power greater than any one of them. A further problem involves the mechanism by which such aggregation as may be possible can in fact be brought about: the consent of the relevant individuals may be a necessary condition for the uniting of their respective powers, but it can hardly be regarded as sufficient. Consent alone does not provide the organization and coordination required for those individuals to be able to act according to a single commanding will. For this reason, what Hobbes describes as the power of a sovereign is an unrealized, and almost certainly as unrealizable, aspiration. Hobbes would be the first to admit that no ruler – particularly in seventeenth-century Europe – is able to make effective use of the powers of all of his or her subjects in the way that his model requires.

The sovereign power that plays such an important part in Hobbes' argument, then, does not describe the 'present means to obtain some future apparent Good' at the disposal of any actual sovereign. It is, in other words, something other than a real and effective *power*, at least in the strict sense of his initial definition.

In fact, Hobbes' discussion of 'sovereign power' is less about *power*, understood in the manner of his definition, than it is about the political constitution of society and the character of government: *the* government is the sovereign, and the *activity* of government is the exercise of sovereign power. By describing the sovereign as constituted through the authorization of its subjects, Hobbes is able to formulate a more general model of sovereign or governmental power both as emanating from a single central intelligence and as operating primarily by means of decisions which its subjects have normally agreed to accept as binding. The significance of Hobbes' model of sovereign power for our purposes lies not so much in the details of his argument as in the fact that features of this model pervade many of the more influential current views of the power and operation of government. It is the elision here between questions of power in the sense of quantitative capacity and questions of power in the sovereign or governmental sense that has prevented power from ever being treated by modern theorists in purely quantitative terms, and so has stifled the apparent empirical promise of the notion.

Hobbes' model of sovereign power presents us with three central assumptions: first, the sovereign, whether it be 'this Man, or . . . this Assembly of Men', is conceived of as a centralized, unitary authority, and is seen as the single most important power operating in a society; secondly, the making of decisions by government, and especially the enactment of laws, is regarded as its most significant activity; thirdly, the subjects who jointly constitute the sovereign power are regarded as having been formed as personalities independently of the activities of government. Much of Hobbes' analysis has been widely disputed. Nevertheless, with the partial exception of the third, these assumptions about what sovereign power is or what it ought to be, have been at the heart of what is now regarded as the tradition of modern political theory.

For the moment, let me briefly illustrate this last point by reference to two of the most important traditions of Western political thought, namely, contract theory and republicanism. While there were earlier versions of the idea that political authority should be understood in contractual terms, the characteristically modern form of contract theory can be described as proposing to consider the legitimacy or otherwise of the institutions of a political community primarily in terms of the idea of free contract between equal and independent individuals.[4] Institutions that could be seen as if they had resulted from such a contract are regarded as legitimate, while those that could not are regarded as illegitimate.

Precisely what otherwise independent individuals might be expected freely to agree to is, of course, a matter of considerable debate amongst contract theorists. While some contractarians maintain that anything more than the most minimal of governments is an unjustifiable form of oppression, others argue for a welfare state and for government action to redistribute income and wealth.[5] Nevertheless, there exists among contractarians a core area of agreement concerning the existence of a political community – without such a community there would be no political institutions to consider in the first place. This political community is analysed as if it had been jointly contracted by otherwise independent individuals. The purposes that contractarians attribute to such contracts vary, but the most important of them is always thought to be mutual protection – the social contract defends its participants against each other as much as against outsiders. On this view, an indispensable task of government is to secure internal peace and security through the enactment of laws, and through creation of the machinery required for enforcement of those laws.

The core ideas of republican thought also have a long ancestry, being traceable back at least to the time of the Roman Republic. Republicanism, in something like its modern form, emerged with the rise of city states in northern Italy towards the end of the Middle Ages. It played an influential role in English political thinking in the mid-seventeenth century, around the time of the Revolution, and later in the American and French Revolutions.[6] Republican ideas have since continued to be highly influential in democratic and socialist political thought.

Republicanism is not to be seen as an alternative, defined in opposition to contract theory. Rather, it is a tradition that addresses a characteristically different set of concerns. Where contract theory assumes that individuals may be regarded as existing in some sense independently of the political community they agree to form, republican thought treats its individuals as citizens – that is, as members of a self-governing political community. Republican thought therefore supposes a considerably more intimate relationship between citizens and the political community or republic to which they belong than does contract theory. Where the latter is concerned to identify the institutions that freely contracting persons might be expected to constitute, the former considers what conditions are required to preserve the liberty of both citizens and community. Nevertheless, republicanism is not necessarily incompatible with the basic assumptions of contract theory. Rousseau's essay *The Social Contract* (1762), for instance, has a place in both traditions (see Rousseau 1968).

The most important feature of the republican tradition to be noted here is the assumption that the liberty of the republic may be threatened not only by the actions of outsiders, but also by the actions of powerful individuals or groups within the community itself. This starting point leads naturally to the argument that preservation of the liberty of citizens depends on their collectively taking responsibility for the liberty of the republic to which they belong. In particular, they should agree to constitute and maintain a collective power greater than that of any individual or faction.

Now consider the three assumptions noted above. In Hobbes' discussion, the first assumption follows directly from the claim that the power of government consists in the totality of the powers of its subjects, brought together under the control of a single guiding intelligence. While many forms of contract theory and of republicanism lack this totalizing conception of sovereign power, the doctrine of its primacy over other powers is a necessary feature of both contractarian and republican analyses of the character of government. If the collective power is to be seen as able to protect its subjects or its citizens against each other, then it must also be regarded as greater than any of them.

As for the second assumption, Hobbes' sovereign power is constituted by a multiplicity of discrete acts of authorization, in each of which an individual assigns to the sovereign 'my Right of Governing my selfe' (*Leviathan*, ch. XVII; 1968, p. 227). Sovereign power operates primarily by means of that right; that is, by commanding the obedient behaviour of its subjects and by calling on the use of their powers. Both contract theory and republicanism also treat governmental power as operating largely through the agreement of individual members of a community to treat the decisions of government as binding, and as operating through the use of force or other forms of coercion only in the event of recalcitrance. As far as internal matters are concerned, then, government activity consists primarily of the issuing of laws and their implementation. This suggests a view of government that is enshrined in the long-standing distinction between the legislature and the executive department of government, which was clearly stated in the *Federalist Papers*:

> The essence of the legislative authority is to enact laws, or, in other words, to prescribe rules for the regulation of society; while the execution of the laws and the employment of the common strength, either for this purpose or for the common defense, seem to comprise all the functions of the executive magistrate. (Madison et al. 1987 [1788] p. 425)

The third assumption is rather more problematic. In the works of Hobbes and other contract theorists, the view that independent individuals agree, at least implicitly, to establish a sovereign power for their mutual protection clearly implies that those individuals are formed as personalities independently of the activities of the sovereign power they agree to constitute. However, in republican doctrine, citizens are regarded as being individually and collectively responsible for preserving the liberty of the community. Both the republic and the citizens within it therefore have a legitimate interest in ensuring that citizens develop appropriate personal qualities and attributes. In this respect, republican thought does not regard citizens as having quite the independence that contract theory accords its individuals. The significance of this point will be made clear in chapter 4.

Everyone knows, of course, that the view of government as a decision-making centre is seriously incomplete: not only does government operate through a variety of dispersed agencies, not all of which are under the direct control of a unified central authority, but also there is far more to government activity than the creating of laws and the issuing of commands. A majority of governments in the world today make an effort to develop certain personal qualities and attributes in their citizens through a variety of means – most obviously through universal compulsory education. In addition, it is generally acknowledged that governments are not the only significant determinants of what happens in their societies, and that they frequently fail to impose their will. However, these obvious facts have not prevented the image of government as a controlling centre whose most important activity consists in the issuing of decisions to its independently formed subjects, from dominating contemporary discussion of political power.

Two examples should serve to illustrate this point. The first relates to Dahl's analysis of democracy, as this is laid out in *Democracy and its Critics* (1989), which represents a lifetime's reflections on the subject. Dahl's central argument is presented in chapter 8, 'A Theory of the Democratic Process', and here a political order is defined in terms of the assumption that a number of persons agree to form an association, or to adapt an existing association to pursue certain ends.

> To achieve these ends, the association needs to adopt policies, with which members will be obliged to act consistently. Ordinarily, their obligation to act consistently with the policies of the association is expressed in a rule or a law that includes penalties for noncompliance. Because members are obliged to obey the rules or laws, the decisions may be said to be *binding*. Taken collectively, the decision makers who make binding decisions constitute the *government* of the association. (Dahl 1989, pp. 106–7)

Dahl's argument here clearly depends on the second and third assumptions found in Hobbes' model of government: it assumes that the defining activity of government is the making of decisions, and especially the enactment of laws, and it treats the persons forming the association as logically prior to the government that they constitute. As for Hobbes' first assumption, Dahl insists that the association can be regarded as democratic – and therefore as legitimately governed – only if all those normally subject to its laws are able to participate as equals, either in the making of binding decisions, or in the appointment of those who make such decisions. It follows that no individual or faction should be in a position simply to impose its preferred decisions on the association: the government should be able to resist the power of any single individual or faction.

The second example returns us to the issues raised in the first part of this chapter. The community power debates of the 1950s were in fact debates about the location of sovereign power, about who makes the big decisions in American society. Mills, like other advocates of the elitist analysis of American society, argues that the rhetoric of democracy in America is misleading, and that the most important decisions are not made by the people or by their elected representatives. Rather, they are made by those with 'access to the command of major institutions' (Mills 1959, p. 9). As well as leading politicians and key government officials, these include 'admirals and generals, and . . . the major owners and executives of the larger corporations' (ibid.). Together they form an elite consisting of 'men whose positions enable them to transcend the ordinary environments of ordinary men and women; they are in a position to make decisions having major consequences' (ibid., pp. 3–4). Since it makes the crucial decisions, Mills regards this power elite as the real government of America.

Likewise, Dahl, while denying that there is a unified elite of the kind that Mills purports to describe in contemporary America, nevertheless agrees that the dispute can be decided only by examining 'a series of concrete decisions. And these decisions must either constitute the universe or a fair sample of the universe of key political decisions taken in the political system' (Dahl 1958, p. 286). The 'key political decisions' here are, of course, those that are or should be taken by government.

In spite of their other differences, then, all participants in the debate take it for granted that what is at issue in the investigation of the distribution of power is the question of 'Who Governs?' (the title of Dahl's own study of community power). Further, all assume that this question is synonymous with 'Who makes the most important decisions?' This set of assumptions takes us beyond questions of the distribution of power in the sense of quantitative capacity. Rather, what is at issue is the possession of sovereign or governmental power.

3

'a Right of making Laws': *Locke on Political Power and Morality*

What contemporary readers are most likely to find disturbing about Hobbes' account of sovereign power is the fact that the sovereign is not a party to the agreement by which its power is established. The sovereign power is constituted by an agreement between those who are to become its subjects, not between those subjects and their sovereign. It is:

> as if every man should say to every man, I Authorise and give up my Right of Governing my selfe, to this Man, or to this Assembly of men, on this condition, that thou give up thy Right to him, and Authorise all his Actions in like manner. (*Leviathan*, ch. XVII; 1968, p. 227)

Several important consequences follow from Hobbes' argument that the sovereign power is constituted by an agreement of this kind. First, as we have seen, he maintains that the sovereign is by far the most powerful person in the society. The relation between sovereign and subject is therefore characterized by an extreme asymmetry of power. Secondly, however, this form of agreement establishes an important asymmetry of another kind. The sovereign power is constituted by Covenant between those who thereby agree to become its subjects, but it is not itself a party to their agreement. While the subjects incur obligations towards the sovereign by virtue of their Covenant, the sovereign incurs no corresponding obligations towards its subjects. In particular, then, the sovereign is in no way bound by the desires or moral concerns of its subjects. Subjects may disagree with the sovereign's actions on moral grounds or other grounds, but their disagreement gives them no right to withhold their allegiance or to replace one sovereign by another. In Hobbes' view of the constitution of sovereignty, then, there is no scope for anyone to question the legitimacy of the rule to which they are subjected.

In contrast to this, Locke's *Second Treatise on Government*[1] presents an influential account of political power in which the holder of that power is regarded as having very definite obligations towards its subjects. Following brief discussions, first, of the Lockean understandings of legitimate and illegitimate power and of tyranny, and secondly, of Locke's treatment of morality, I will suggest that a broadly Lockean view of political power and a corresponding style of political critique have played, and continue to play, a major role in Western political thought.

Power, Usurpation and Tyranny

Locke sets out what he understands by political power at the beginning of his *Second Treatise on Government*. It is:

> a *Right* of making Laws with Penalties of Death, and consequently all less Penalties, for the Regulating and Preserving of Property, and of employing the force of the Community, in the execution of such Laws, and

in the defence of the Common-wealth from Foreign Injury, and all this only for the Publick Good. (§3; 1988, p. 268)[2]

Political power in this sense is the power of a sovereign over its subjects. Locke insists that it should be distinguished from the respective powers of 'a *Father* over his Children, a *Master* over his Servant, a *Husband* over his Wife, and a *Lord* over his Slave' (§2; 1988, p. 268).

This view of political power has a number of interesting features. First, it undermines two influential kinds of apologia for the pretence of kings to absolute power. Locke insists that political power should be understood in terms of the distinctive character of the government of a political community and, in particular, that it cannot be justified by analogy either with the rights of the master over his household or with the kind of power (over a slave) that may be obtained through conquest. As to the first, Locke goes on to argue that the powers of a master (or indeed of a mistress) over other members of a household are themselves strictly limited. Paternal power, for example, is nothing more than the power a parent has over a child. It might 'be more properly called *Parental Power*' (§52; 1988, p. 303). Locke maintains that while all men have an equal right to their natural freedom, parental power is necessary because they are born 'ignorant and without the use of *Reason*' (§57; 1988, p. 305). On this view, the rights that parents have to rule over their children may be justified only by the fact that the latter are not yet able to govern themselves. In normal circumstances parental rights will be strictly temporary, lasting until the child attains the age of reason. The analogy with parental power, then, can hardly be invoked to support the claim to exercise power over those who do have the use of their reason.

However, a natural corollary of this justification for the exercise of parental power is the suggestion that other persons who are thought to be without the use of reason might also benefit from remaining under the government of others. Locke's defence of the power of a parent, then, might also be used in support of other kinds of paternalism.[3] Nevertheless, the strictly temporary and limited character of parental power ensures that, even if a parallel were to be drawn between the power of a father and that of a king, it would not be able to sustain the royal claim to absolute power.

As for the power that might be obtained through conquest, Locke describes the condition of slavery as a relation 'between a lawful Conqueror, and a Captive' (§24; 1988, p. 284). The notion of a *lawful* conqueror is crucial to Locke's understanding of the kind of power that is involved in slavery. In his view, all men have a right to their natural freedom under the Law of Nature. It follows that they cannot lawfully be deprived of that freedom unless they have forfeited their rights under the Law of Nature. This happens, he suggests, when one person attempts to deprive others of their natural freedom or of their property. The aggressor who attempts to take away my freedom 'puts himself into a State of War with me' (§17; 1988, p. 279). He therefore forfeits the protection of his life and his freedom under the Law of Nature.

Locke's account of slavery has two important implications for his view of relations between rulers and subjects. One is that any ruler who makes a claim to absolute power threatens the natural freedom of his subjects, and therefore puts himself into a state of war with them. They have a right to resist and, if necessary, to kill him. The other implication is that the condition of slavery can apply only to those persons who have placed themselves in a state of war, thereby forfeiting their natural rights. Lawful conquest gives the conquerors rights only over the conquered themselves. In particular, it gives no lawful powers over the children of the conquered. Conquest, then, is not a legitimate foundation for political power.

Now consider Locke's definition of political power as a *right*. It does not accord with Hobbes' definition in which power is presented as a capacity to achieve one's objectives – although, as we have seen, the view of power as a right is an integral part of Hobbes' understanding of sovereign power. Nor does the idea of political power as a right seem to accord with Locke's own treatment of the general concept of power in *An Essay Concerning Human Understanding*. Power as a right is an attribute of relations between persons. In contrast, the *Essay* presents a version of the Platonic view of power as an ability to affect or to be affected by something else. On this latter view, power should be seen as an attribute of substance, and specifically as the capacity of a substance to modify or to be modified by others: 'Fire has a *power* to melt Gold . . . and Gold has a *power* to be melted' (*Essay*, Book II, ch. XXI, §1; 1957, p. 233). It is in something like this sense that we might refer to the power of a detergent or an antibiotic.[4] People certainly have powers of this kind (Locke gives the examples of will and liberty), but political power considered as a *right*, and all the parental and other powers that Locke insists should not be confused with political power, are not among them. These political and other such powers are what concern us here.

In fact, closer inspection of Locke's *Second Treatise on Government* suggests that his opening specification of political power as a *right* is misleading. While the *Second Treatise* begins with the definition of political power quoted above, it goes on to consider cases in which political power is assumed to be something rather different. He uses the term 'usurpation', for example, to refer to conditions in which political power is exercised by those who have no right to it. This suggests that the *power* that is under discussion here is not so much 'a *right* of making laws [etc.] . . . for the Publick Good' as it is an effective *capacity* to impose laws and to employ 'the force of the Community': the right to do these things is of little value if the necessary capacity has been usurped by another. Political power, in Locke's sense, acts primarily through making laws and enforcing them and defending the commonwealth from injury. That power is legitimate if those who have the capacity also have the right.

Locke's use of the notion of political power as referring to both right and capacity suggests two ways in which questions to do with the legitimacy of such power might arise. First, political power may be exercised by those with no right to it. Secondly, that power may be used for purposes other than the public good.

> As Usurpation is the exercise of Power, which another hath a Right to; so Tyranny is the exercise of Power beyond Right, which no Body can have a Right to. And this is making use of the Power any one has in his hands; not for the good of those who are under it, but for his own private separate Advantage. When the Governour, however intituled, makes not the Law, but his Will, the Rule; and his Commands and Actions are not directed to the preservation of the Properties of his People, but the satisfaction of his own Ambition, Revenge, Covetousness, or any other irregular Passion. (*Second Treatise*, §199; 1988, pp. 398–9)

This notion of power as a right that may be exercised only for the public good allows Locke to identify cases in which the people may refuse allegiance to their rulers. Unlike Hobbes, Locke is entirely prepared to justify the right of rebellion: the community may remove an illegitimate government and replace it with another.

The crucial question here, of course, is who should decide whether a government is legitimate – that is, whether it holds power as a *right* or whether, on the contrary, its power has been usurped or is tyrannical. Locke's answer is clear: the decision must rest with the people themselves, not with their government. This is also the view of government set out in the second paragraph of the American Declaration of Independence:

> that to secure these rights governments are instituted among men, deriving their just powers from the consent of the governed; that whenever any form of government becomes destructive of these ends, *it is the right of the people to alter or to abolish it*, and to institute new government. (emphasis added)

To the suggestion that this doctrine would licence political instability and frequent rebellion, and should for that reason be regarded as dangerous, Locke responds:

> many wrong and inconvenient Laws, and all the slips of humane frailty will be *born by the People*, without mutiny or murmer. But if a long train of Abuses, Prevarications, and Artifices, all tending the same way,[5] make the design visible to the People, and they cannot but feel, what they lie under, and see, whither they are going; 'tis not to be wonder'd, that they should then rouze themselves, and endeavour to put the rule into such hands, which may secure to them the ends for which Government was at first erected . . . (*Second Treatise*, §225; 1988, p. 415)

In fact, Locke argues, the doctrine that the people may remove a government that has acted contrary to their trust is *'the best fence against Rebellion,* and the probablest means to hinder it' (ibid., §226; 1988, p. 415).

I noted at the beginning of this chapter that on Hobbes' account of sovereignty, no question of the legitimacy of an established sovereign power can possibly arise. In Hobbes' view, natural law gives individuals a right to resist should the sovereign threaten their lives, but otherwise they should treat the sovereign's instructions as their own. They certainly have no right to remove a sovereign and put another in its place.

However, there is more to the difference between Hobbes and Locke on this point than the simple matter of a right to rebellion. In Hobbes' account, the covenant establishes a commonwealth by constituting a sovereign power to rule over it. To remove the sovereign would therefore be to dissolve the commonwealth, thereby plunging the people back into the state of war of all against all which their covenant was intended to replace. What Locke's argument requires if it is to avoid that conclusion is a distinction between

> the *Dissolution of the Society,* and the *Dissolution of the Government.* That which makes the Community, and brings Men out of the loose State of Nature, into one *Politick Society,* is the Agreement which every one has with the rest to incorporate, and act as one Body, and so be one distinct Commonwealth. (*Second Treatise,* §211; 1988, p. 406)

If the society ceases to exist, then its government cannot continue. However, the reverse is not the case. Governments may be 'dissolved from within' (ibid., §212; 1988,

p. 407), leaving the society intact. In effect, two kinds of contract are involved in Locke's account of political power as a right. One establishes the commonwealth and the other constitutes the relationship between a commonwealth and its government. Locke writes of the latter as if it had the character of a trust. Thus governments may be dissolved when they act contrary to their trust, in which case 'they forfeit the Power, the People had put into their hands, for quite contrary ends, and it devolves to the People . . . (ibid., §222; 1988, p. 412). In effect, then, this conception of political power as a right involves a corresponding view of the rights of those who are subject to the exercise of such power.

Power as Right and as Capacity

I argued in chapter two that Hobbes' concept of sovereign power involves a slippage between the idea of power as a *capacity* to act and that of power as a *right*. While his formal definition of power is a version of the first, his account of the constitution of sovereign power through numerous acts of authorization clearly implies the second. We have now seen that a similar slippage (in the reverse direction) appears in Locke's account of political power. Before continuing with the discussion of Locke it should be noted that such slippages between the idea of power as capacity and the idea of power as right have been a widespread feature of Western political thought in the modern period. They arise from the understanding of political (or sovereign) power as a distinctive kind of capacity to act – one that is normally supposed to work by calling on the performance of pre-existing obligations.

Perhaps the most influential versions of this conception of political power in the modern period are those based on the idea that sovereignty itself is founded in a social contract. Contract theorists are far from being committed to the view that such a contract is an identifiable historical event. What matters for their arguments is that the *idea* of the contract serves both as the basis of the legitimacy of sovereign power – and therefore, at least in some accounts, as the basis on which the actions of the sovereign may be disputed[6] – and as the key to the effectiveness of such a power. Thus, on the one hand, the contract appears to give the sovereign the right to govern and, on the other, to the extent that the subjects can be relied on to obey their sovereign's legitimate instructions, it also gives the sovereign the capacity to do so. A power that is said to be based on contract will be thought to work primarily by calling on others to fulfil their obligations. It can do this either through general rules (laws) or through particularized commands – although there can always be other means of action in the background.

The conception of power as combining a right and a correlative means of acting plays a central role in modern discussions of government, but it may also be employed in other contexts. The real or implied contract of employment, for example, is usually understood as establishing a right on the part of the employer to issue instructions across a certain range of activities, and a corresponding obligation on the part of the employee to obey. What is involved in these cases, governmental or otherwise, is a view of the relation between ruler and ruled as if it could normally be seen as a matter of right, consent and obligation. Power relations would then appear to be a matter, on the one side, of those who make the rules and, on the other, of those who have agreed to obey them and who, in the event of recalcitrance, may be compelled to do so. This, in turn, requires a perception of the ruled as individuals who could normally be regarded as endowed, with, first the legal and the mental capacity to give or to withhold their rational consent, and, secondly, with the ability to act on those obligations which their real or implied consent might entail.

If the ruler is a government, this amounts to a view of the political constitution of society and the proper relationship between government and citizen, and a corresponding understanding of the legal and moral capacities of its citizens/subjects. It also suggests that the most important activities of government – at least with regard to the internal affairs of the community – are the making and enforcing of rules. As we shall see, such a view of government also suggests a strong case for treating the personal qualities and attributes of individual citizens as if they were matters of public concern and, if necessary, of public intervention.

We shall see in chapter 5 that this view of government is in marked contrast to the Foucauldian account of government. As Foucault presents it, the most general problem of government is how to conduct the conduct of others. He notes that contract theory

> enables the founding contract, the mutual pledge of ruler and subjects, to function as a sort of theoretical matrix for deriving the general principles of an art of government. (Foucault 1991, p. 98)

However, he also notes that the idea of a power that is based on, and operates through, the consent of its subjects must be regarded, at best, as providing an answer of a remarkably limited kind – albeit one that has been extraordinarily influential in modern political theory. This answer is limited if only because, at least in the first instance, consent provides the answer to a radically different question: namely, what is the basis of the legitimacy of sovereign power? The slippage which exists between the idea of power as a right and the idea of power as a capacity, then, allows the answer to the question of legitimacy to appear as if it could also stand as an answer to the problem of government.

The Law of Opinion and Reputation

The Lockean view of political power as involving the execution of a trust lays the foundations for a radical critique of political power that has been remarkably influential in the democratic and the liberal traditions of politics in the modern West. The primary concern of this critique is not so much with the empirical question of who has power in a particular community or society, but rather with questions about the legitimacy of that power: whether those who exercise political power have a right to its possession, and whether they employ it for legitimate ends. However, there is one further aspect of Locke's political thought that must be considered before the full significance of this modern critique can be appreciated. This concerns the political significance of morality.

We can best approach this issue by considering Locke's treatment of morality in chapter XXVIII of Book II of *An Essay Concerning Human Understanding*. Having argued that what we call good and evil are merely whatever occasions pleasure and pain, Locke goes on to describe *morally* good and *morally* evil as a matter of conformity or non-conformity 'of our Actions to some Law, whereby Good or Evil is drawn on us, from the Will and Power of the Law-maker' (Book II, ch. XXVIII, §5; 1957, p. 351). Locke writes of three kinds of law, each with its own manner of enforcement and its own types of reward and punishment: the Divine Law, the Civil Law, and the 'Law of Opinion or Reputation', which Locke also calls 'Philosophical Law' (ibid., §10; 1957, p. 353). Morality is a matter of conformity to one or other of these Laws, but it is the second and third that particularly concern us here. Civil law is the law invoked in Locke's definition of political power, and we have seen that it plays an important part in the argument of his *Two Treatises of Govern-*

ment. Political power is the right of making civil law, and civil law in turn is the principal means of action of political power, that is, of government. Political power is also the source of juridical regulation and punishment. The 'Law of Opinion or Reputation', on the other hand, plays no part in the argument of the *Treatises*. In describing this law in his *Essay*, Locke maintains that what people regard as virtue or vice should not be understood as a matter of actions that are right or wrong in themselves, since what is considered a vice in one country may be considered a virtue (or at least not a vice) in another. Rather, these terms refer to actions that are regarded as worthy of praise or blame in the community in question. The content of this law is established by approbation and dislike.

> For though Men uniting into politick Societies, have resigned up to the publick the disposing of all their Force, so that they cannot employ it against any Fellow-Citizen, any farther than the Law of the Country directs: yet they retain still the power of Thinking well or ill; approving or disapproving of the actions of those whom they live amongst, and converse with. (*Essay*, §10; 1957, p. 353)

Why does Locke write of a '*Law* of Opinion or Reputation', when law always requires a power to enforce it? His answer is that 'he, who imagines Commendation and Disgrace, not to be strong Motives on Men. . . . seems little skill'd in the Nature, or History of Mankind' (ibid., §12; 1957, pp. 356–7). The law of opinion, in other words, is enforced extremely effectively. In fact, Locke insists that most communities are governed by the law of opinion, and that this is more directly effective in the regulation of behaviour than the laws of God and the commonwealth. People give little thought to the first, and they often imagine themselves immune to the second.

> But no Man scapes the Punishment of their Censure and Dislike, who offends against the Fashion and Opinion of the Company he keeps, and would recommend himself to. Nor is there one of ten thousand, who is stiff and insensible enough, to bear up under the constant Dislike, and Condemnation of his own Club. (*Essay*, §12; 1957, p. 357)

Locke's point is not that there is any necessary conflict between these different kinds of law, since he also maintains that the divine law and the law of opinion will normally coincide. His point is simply that they have distinct sources and means of enforcement.

Locke's discussion of the three laws and their respective modes of enforcement has important implications for the regulation (or government) of human conduct which I take up in chapter 4. What concerns us at this point is how morality bears on considerations of the legitimacy of political power. We have seen that in Hobbes' view the moral concerns of the subjects can have no bearing on their obligations to their sovereign. Locke, on the other hand, describes morality as having a definite public or social quality. In particular, he suggests that the moral standards that arise out of everyday social interaction have the character of laws. Unlike the laws laid down by government, they are formed by the 'secret and tacite consent' (*Essay*, §10; 1957, p. 353) of individual members of the community; that is, they are formed without requiring the blessing or the authorization of their rulers. I return to the significance of this point in a moment.

What does this account of morality imply for the relationship between government and morality? We have seen that political power, the power of a government, is the capacity to make and enforce laws and to employ the force of a community, and that government itself has the character of a trust. On this view, political power is ultimately answerable to the people. Where political power is legitimate, then, both civil law and the law of opinion and reputation could be seen as emanating from the people: the one enacted by government in the execution of its trust, and the other arising from the 'secret and tacite consent' of the people themselves. Locke does not directly address the question of how these two kinds of law might be related. However, in the light of his comments (noted above) on the divine law and the law of opinion and reputation, it seems reasonable to expect that they would broadly coincide.

Are there conditions under which civil law and the law of opinion might not coincide? Where political power has been usurped or used tyrannically, the sphere of morality defined by civil law is likely to reflect what Locke's *Second Treatise* calls the 'private separate Advantage' (§199; 1988, p. 399) of the governors rather than the good of the people. Under those conditions the injunctions of civil law may well deviate from those of the law of opinion and reputation. In such cases the civil law could hardly be trusted to provide an independent basis for deciding on the legitimacy either of a government or of its particular actions. These matters must be decided, then, by reference to laws of other kinds, that is, by reference to the divine law or the law of opinion. While Locke affirms that the former 'is the only true touchstone of *moral Rectitude*' (*Second Treatise*, Book II, ch. XXVIII, §8; 1988, p. 352) he also insists that the latter is the more influential in practice. It seems, then, that the law of opinion and reputation should be seen as an important source of the moral foundations on which the people might judge the legitimacy or otherwise of political power.

There is a further significant point to be noted here, which is that moral foundations of this kind cannot be regarded as having been fashioned or imposed by any central authority. Rather, they are based on a morality that arises out of the normal life of society, one that is generated and sustained in the daily interactions and discussions occurring in associations and clubs, coffee houses and bars, and other arenas of public life. In other words, this morality arises out of what later became known as civil society. This idea of civil society will be considered at greater length in chapter 4. For the moment, it is sufficient to point out that in this later usage the term refers to those aspects of social life which lie outside the realm of direct state or government activity: if civil society is to be able to provide the moral foundations on which the people might assess the legitimacy of their government, then it must be free from control by that government.

In many respects the idea of political power occupies a similar place in Locke's account of government as the idea of sovereign power does in Hobbes' account. First, Locke presents political power as the single most important power operating in a society and he assigns to its possessor responsibility for external defence. Secondly, apart from defence, he assumes that the most significant activities of political power are the enactment and enforcement of laws. Thirdly, at least in his *Two Treatises*, Locke treats subjects as having been formed as personalities (and as *moral* personalities in particular) independently of the activities of government.

Nevertheless, there are also fundamental differences between these two perspectives on political or sovereign power. We have seen that the Hobbesian account of sovereignty denies the right of rebellion, since subjects are said to have no contractual rights with respect to the sovereign power. Hobbes also maintains that the sovereign need not be constrained by the moral concerns of its subjects. Here, sovereign power as right is understood in some absolute sense. Locke disputes both of these positions. His account of government clearly allows the people the right of rebellion, while his account of morality can be read as suggesting that their 'secret and tacite consent' provides the moral foundations on which the legitimacy of their government might be judged. For Locke, political power is regarded as legitimate only if it rests on the right of the people to withdraw their consent. This view of political power is a central presupposition of modern democratic thought.

The Community Power Debate Reconsidered

In Britain after 1689, and in the independent United States of America, it was possible for supporters of Lockean principles of government to argue that constitutional mechanisms were already in place whereby government could be subordinated to the will of the people, and if necessary replaced. This was not the case in the greater part of continental Europe throughout the eighteenth century, and in many cases throughout the nineteenth century as well. Koselleck (1988) has argued that the absolutist state provided the conditions of political stability within which the Enlightenment ideal of a life based on reason could flourish. However, it also maintained a dichotomy between subject and sovereign, between the private morality of philosophical law on the one side and the public policy of government on the other. Koselleck suggests that under these conditions, Lockean ideas of government and of morality provided the foundations for a moral critique of established political power which was elaborated both in the writings of Enlightenment philosophers and in the activities of such groups as the Freemasons, the Illuminati and the Republic of Letters throughout the eighteenth century.

Koselleck's aim in *Critique and Crisis* (1988) is to clarify an influential style of thinking about politics, and to identify some of the conditions under which it was able to develop. What should be noted here is that echoes of this eighteenth-century Lockean critique of political power can readily be found in more recent developments. For example, the idea of the moral and political significance of an autonomous civil society, free of interference from the state, emerged as an important element in East European political discussion in the period leading up to the collapse of communist rule in 1989–90. It has also been taken up, for rather different reasons, by socialist thinkers in the West.[7] I return to this point in the following chapter as part of a discussion of that offshoot of Marxism now known as critical theory.

As a rather different example, consider the broadly Lockean understanding of the relationship between political power and the consent of the governed that is incorporated in the American Declaration of Independence. It seems clear that such an understanding of political power was taken for granted by participants in the community power debates of the 1950s and 1960s. Thus, those who argued that American society was ruled by elites, at either the local or the national level, were concerned with what Locke interpreted as the usurpation of political power. Hunter, for instance, begins his study of power in Atlanta with the statement that the character of relations between governors and governed 'does not square with the concept of democracy we have been taught to revere' (Hunter 1953, p. 1). Or again, Mills, writing in *The Power Elite* about American society as a whole, maintains that:

The top of the American system of power is much more unified and much more powerful, the bottom is much more fragmented, and in truth, impotent,

than is generally supposed by those who are distracted by the middling units of power which neither
express such will as exists at the bottom nor determine the decisions at the top. (Mills 1959, p. 29)

These 'middling units of power' include political parties,
pressure groups and other political organizations, all of
which are normally supposed to mediate between the
governors and the governed in a democratic society –
thereby ensuring that political power does indeed rest on
the consent of the governed. Because, according to Mills,
these middling units do not, in fact, perform that role, he
concludes that the holders of power

are not men shaped by nationally responsible parties
that debate openly and clearly the issues this nation
now so unintelligently confronts. They are not men
held in responsible check by a plurality of voluntary
associations which connect debating publics with
the pinnacles of decision. Commanders of power
unequalled in human history, they have succeeded
within the American system of organised irresponsibility. (Mills 1959, p. 361)

On this view, political power in America is irresponsible
– and indeed illegitimate – because it is not securely
based in the consent of the people.

Parsons' claim – in his hostile review of *The Power
Elite* (Parsons 1969b) – that Mills tends to treat power as
presumptively illegitimate, can thus be seen to be misplaced. Power itself is presumed to be no more, and no
less, illegitimate in Mills' analysis than political power is
presumed to be in Locke's *Two Treatises on Government*. Mills' objection is not to power as such, but rather
to the fact that, as he sees it, power is not in the hands
of the people. Furthermore, as the Lockean account of

morality would lead us to expect, there is a strong presumption in Mills' argument that illegitimate power is also immoral.

Subsequent discussions of power have tended to concentrate on Dahl's powerful methodological critique of the empirical claims of the ruling elite model (Dahl 1958), and on the elite theorists' response, and to have overlooked their shared concern with political power as a *right* – thereby giving the misleading impression that Dahl's critique of elite theory amounts to an endorsement of the American political system. In fact, while Dahl's study of New Haven politics, *Who Governs? democracy and power in an American city*, argues that New Haven is no longer ruled by an elite, he nevertheless acknowledges that the political system of New Haven is

> a long way from achieving the goal of political equality advocated by the philosophers of democracy and incorporated into the creed of democracy and equality practically every American professes to uphold. (Dahl 1961, p. 86)

However, in marked contrast to the elite theorists, Dahl does not treat that fact as if it were *prima facie* evidence of the illegitimacy (or the immorality) of those who hold power. Rather, his response is to argue that the model of relations between rulers and ruled has to be modified to take account of the complexity of public life in America and other 'democratic' societies. Yet, his conclusion that 'New Haven is a republic of unequal citizens – but for all that a republic' (Dahl 1961, p. 220) is far from being an unequivocal endorsement of the American system of political power. It suggests that the people do rule, but that they rule in a fashion that is not properly 'democratic'.

Both sides in this debate take it for granted that political power should be strictly limited and conditional on the right of the people to withdraw their consent. Despite appearances, what is at issue between the elite theorists and their opponents is not the question of the empirical location of political power, but rather the question of its *legitimacy*: whether or not such power is rightfully held.

4

'the supreme exercise of power':
Lukes and Critical Theory

In *Power: a radical view* (1974), Lukes contrasts his own 'radical' perspective with the 'liberal' account of power presented by Dahl and other American pluralists and also with the 'reformist' view presented by many of their critics. While Lukes describes the pluralists as insisting that the exercise of power can be identified only in cases of observable conflict, he sees their 'reformist' critics as recognizing that power may also be exercised in such a way as to prevent certain conflicts of interest from appearing in the political arena. Both views, in other words, regard power as enabling some individuals or groups to prevail over others in situations where there are clear differences between what they would identify as their respective interests. Lukes goes further to advance the 'radical' view that power can also operate to prevent such differences from emerging in the first place, and that it does so by ensuring that those subject to its influence have a false understanding of where their true interests lie. In such cases, power works by manipulating the thoughts of its victims:

> is it not the supreme exercise of power to get another or others to have the desires you want them to have – that is, to secure their compliance by controlling their thoughts and desires? (Lukes 1974, p. 23)

[68]

Parents and educators throughout the world attempt to manipulate the thoughts and desires of others as a matter of course. These activities, however, would hardly count as instances of the kind of supreme and objectionable exercise of power that Lukes has in mind, if only because they could be regarded, at least in principle, as serving the interests of their charges. They are examples of Locke's 'parental' power, working only for a limited period and designed to promote the independence of those over whom it is exercised. Lukes' 'radical' view is concerned with what he sees as those more sinister cases in which the power to control the thoughts of others is used against the interests of its victims. Brain-washing would be one example, but in this case power operates on single individuals or small groups and, at least in the early stages of the process, the victims are usually in no doubt that power is being exercised over them. The more insidious and, on Lukes' account, the more significant cases are those in which power is directed not so much at individuals, but rather at 'socially structured and culturally patterned behaviour' (Lukes 1974, p. 22). These are cases in which the exercise of power will often not be recognized by those who are subject to its effects: it affects the thoughts and desires of individuals, but it does so primarily through the action of 'collective forces and social arrangements' (ibid.).

This 'radical' view encapsulates an approach to the analysis of power that has been extremely influential in the modern period. It can be found, for instance, in the belief – widespread amongst Marxists and other socialists – that capitalist society imposes a false consciousness on the working class, and in those feminist arguments which suggest that patriarchy manifests itself not only in legal and institutional arrangements working to the advantage of men, but also in the formation of the consciousnesses of gendered subjects. Other versions have been elaborated in critical theory, which I consider below, and in forms of cultural analysis making use of the Gramscian notion of hegemony.

How does this 'radical' view of power relate to the conceptions of power considered in my earlier chapters? It should be distinguished from the understanding of power as a quantitative capacity considered in chapter 2, since that view does not present power as a matter of controlling the *thoughts* of others. Rather, the capacity that is at issue there concerns the ability of one or more actors to secure their objectives even, as Weber insists, 'against the resistance of others who are participating in the action' (Weber 1978, p. 926). The reference to the possibility of resistance here clearly suggests that the thoughts and desires of those who might engage in such resistance are not themselves determined by the exercise of power in question. On this view, then, actors' thoughts and desires are regarded as setting the parameters within which power may be exercised, not as if they were among the most important of its effects.

The situation with regard to conceptions of political or sovereign power is considerably more complex. In Hobbes' view, the *thoughts* of its subjects are of no interest to the sovereign; what matters is their behaviour. Accordingly, *Leviathan* makes the case for a sovereign who is so overwhelmingly powerful that its subjects, whatever their own opinions, will normally do as they are told. However, in addition to *Leviathan*, I also referred to the tradition of republican political thought as representing the idea that government exercises power over its subjects primarily through the formulation and enforcement of rules. The republic is conceived of as a self-governing political community, that is to say, as a community able to appoint a government of its choosing and to replace that government if it fails in its obligations. It is also regarded as a community of citizens, of free and independent persons endowed with rights which it is the duty of government to preserve. In this respect, the argument of Locke's *Two Treatises* is a republican argument. His discussion makes it clear that political power may be considered legitimate only if the community is able to appoint, and to remove, those who exercise that power. Locke also insists that the main purpose of political power is to protect the life and property of its citizens.

What is of interest here is that republican thought suggests that government should be concerned with the attributes and personal qualities of its subjects – and therefore with at least some of their thoughts and desires. The idea that the political community takes the form of a republic supposes first of all that citizens can participate in the political life of the community. Their participation ensures that the interests of all citizens are represented in its government, but it also serves another purpose: to defend the republic from internal and external threats. The most important internal threat is considered to be that of corruption, either of public officials or of the people. In republican discourse 'corruption' refers to a condition in which individuals pursue their own private interests, to the neglect of the interests of the community as a whole: corrupt officials will undermine legitimate government, while a corrupt people will be governed by the most powerful sectional interests. As for external threats, republican thinkers normally suggest that all citizens have a duty to participate in the defence of the republic. These ideas played an important part in the English revolution, and later in the public life of revolutionary France, of England's North American colonies and then in the United States. The idea of a citizen army remained influential in the Western democracies until well into the second half of the twentieth century.

In the republican view, then, the participation of citizens in the public life of the community is more than just a right. It is also an important duty, since it serves the interests of the community as a whole. It follows that the well-being of the community depends in part on the personal qualities of its citizens. The republic has an interest in ensuring that all citizens develop and maintain appropriate personal qualities and capacities. While contemporary Western societies could hardly be regarded as republics in the classical sense, we nevertheless find that the provision of health, education and training are commonly regarded as matters of particular public concern – partly for reasons to do with the supposed rights of individual citizens, but partly also because of the capacities that are thought to be required if those individuals are to be able to meet the needs of their society.

In this respect, the vision of the republic as a self-governing community of citizens provides powerful reasons why the republic might wish to interfere in the lives of its citizens: for the good of the community as a whole. What is of interest for the present discussion is the relation between, on the one hand, the idea of the citizen as an independent agent, and, on the other, the argument that government should promote the development of suitable capacities and attributes on the part of its citizens for the good of each of them and for the collective good of the entire citizenry. Citizens are regarded both as free and independent agents and as potentially subject to government regulation of their characters. On this view, government *should* be concerned to influence the thoughts and desires of its subjects in certain respects. It seems clear, however, that Lukes would not regard such influence as exemplifying the 'supreme exercise of power' to which he so clearly objects. His objection is not to shaping the thoughts and desires of others so that they are enabled to recognize and act on their own interests. What is objectionable, rather, is the shaping of thoughts and desires so that people misrecognize, and therefore act 'freely' in ways that run counter to, their interests. Lukes suggests that collective decision-making under conditions of democratic participation would avoid that danger (Lukes 1974, p. 33).

In fact, the 'radical' view of power presented in Lukes' book and, in rather more complex form, in critical theory, rests on two fundamental components that play no part in the discourses of power we have considered up to this point. One is the bringing together of the two potentially conflicting conceptions of the human individual noted above: as autonomous rational agent on the one hand and as malleable creature of social conditions on the other. I discuss this in the following section. The other component, which I examine in the second section, is the conception of civil society – the principal field of operation of Locke's law of opinion and reputation – as an arena of contending social forces. The final section of this chapter considers these two components together, using the work of Marcuse and Habermas to show how they have been combined to produce the view of power as an insidious force affecting the thoughts and desires of its victims.

The Government of Behaviour

We have seen that Locke's account of political power gives particularly clear expression to the theme of the individual as autonomous, rational agent. However, his work also provides a useful starting point for discussion of the complementary theme of governmental regulation of the capacities and attributes of the individual as subject. Locke's discussion of political and other forms of power in the *Two Treatises* is crucially dependent on a view of the human individual as the free and independent citizen of republican rhetoric, but his *Essay*

presents a more complex view. Chapter 3 considered
Locke's discussion of political and other forms of power
in the *Two Treatises*. We saw there that his distinction
between political power and paternal (or parental) power
turns on a view of human individuals first as endowed
with a right to their natural freedom but also, secondly,
as born 'ignorant and without the use of *Reason*' (*Two
Treatises*, §57; 1988, p. 305). On this view, paternal
power finds its justification only in the need for a period
of learning and maturation, during which human individuals would normally be expected to acquire the use
of reason. Until they have done so, it is in their interests
that they be guided by others (normally by their parents), and that they be subject to the control of those
others.

In the paradigm case, then, paternal power should have
a strictly temporary character. It can be exercised legitimately only over those who have yet to attain the state of
natural freedom. It is a form of power that does not
require the rational consent of those who are subject to
it, since, by definition, they do not have the full use of
their reason. Otherwise, in Locke's view, where the use
of reason is not in doubt, the legitimate exercise of power
presupposes the rational consent of its subjects – except
where those subjects have forfeited their natural right to
freedom by threatening the freedom of others. Political
power, unlike the power of a parent or the power of a
master over a slave, should rest on the rational consent
of the governed.

Locke's discussion of political power, and his analysis
of the conditions under which it may be regarded as
legitimate, thus depends on a view of the human individual as naturally endowed with a faculty of reason, but
a faculty of reason whose realization requires a suitable
process of learning and maturation. The argument of the
Two Treatises takes it for granted that human adults of

the kind whose government is under discussion will normally have attained the use of that faculty.

Now consider the picture of the human individual presented by Locke's *Essay*. We have seen that, in his discussion of morality, Locke analyses our understandings of good and evil as if they were a function of whatever occasions pleasure or pain. Not all goods, of course, are morally good, and not all evils, morally evil. What qualifies them as *morally* good or evil is a matter of conformity or non-conformity 'of our Actions to some Law, whereby Good or Evil is drawn on us, from the Will and Power of the Law-maker' (*Essay*, Book II, ch. XXVIII, §5; 1957, p. 351). The most influential of these laws is the law of opinion or reputation, whose sanctions consist in expressions of approval or disapproval by one's peers. Our moral understandings of good and evil, then, are consequences of the habits induced by interaction with our peers, and with other sources of reward and sanction. They are products of conditioning, not of any natural inclination towards the good.

Locke applies this same analysis to the ideas to which we give assent in other areas, to our views of what is true or false, beautiful or ugly. While he maintains that we *should* give assent to propositions only after careful consideration of the relevant arguments and the weighing up of evidence, he also insists that there is nothing natural about the adoption of such procedures. Far from being guided by a natural tendency to seek the truth, he argues, we give our assent on the basis of whatever habits of thought have been induced in us by custom, convention and education:

> It is easy to imagine, *how* by these means it comes to pass, that *Men* worship the Idols that have been set up in their Minds; grow fond of Notions they have been long acquainted with there; and *stamp the*

Characters of Divinity, upon Absurdities and Errors, become zealous Votaries to Bulls and Monkeys; and contend too, fight, and die in defence of their Opinions. (*Essay*, Book I, ch. III, §26; 1957, p. 83)

The normal human individuals who emerge from this account are considerably less robust figures than those bearers of a natural right to freedom who play such an important role in the argument of the *Two Treatises of Government*. The latter are presented to us as if they were essentially rational agents, capable of managing their lives according to the dictates of reason – and therefore as if there could be no grounds for denying their capacity to grant or to withhold their rational consent to government. In contrast, the individuals presented to us in the *Essay* are creatures of their society and, in particular, of whatever habits of thought may have been formed both through their education and through their regular interaction with others. In the first place, Locke suggests that if individuals have acquired the proper use of reason, this is not simply because they have been able to grow to maturity under the care of an essentially benign parental power, as the discussion in the *Two Treatises* might at first sight seem to suggest: it is also because they have been subjected to careful training in the appropriate habits of thought. In particular, they must have developed the capacity 'to suspend the prosecution of this or that desire . . . [so that] we have opportunity to examine, view and judge of the good or evil of what we are going to do' (*Essay*, Book II, ch. XXI, §47; 1957, p. 263). Secondly, once having attained the use of their reason, individuals can be expected to retain it only if their habits of rational thought are themselves sustained by the workings of the law of opinion and reputation; that is, only if those habits of thought are shared by those with whom they normally interact. Except in the most rudimentary sense then, rationality should not be regarded as a natural attribute of these creatures.

What should be noted here is that there is far more to the *Essay*'s treatment of our understanding of what is good or evil, true or false, than an exercise in epistemology. Locke's discussion also has significant political implications. One of them is taken up in Koselleck's argument, introduced in chapter 3. Koselleck suggests that, under conditions of absolutist rule, those who imagined themselves to be rational agents of the kind postulated in Locke's *Second Treatise* could read Locke's discussion of the law of opinion and reputation as indicating that their shared beliefs constituted a public moral foundation on which the actions of their rulers might be judged. This view of the public character of morality combined with the Lockean view of governmental legitimacy to provide the bourgeois intelligentsia with the foundations of an influential moral critique of political power.

However, if the *Essay* offers the bourgeois intelligentsia grounds on which they might judge their rulers, it also provides them with means of accounting for the condition of all those persons, in their own and in other societies, whose habits of thought and behaviour seemed to depart from their preferred standards of civilized behaviour. In this respect, the most significant feature of the *Essay* lies in the picture it presents of human subjects as creatures of their habits rather than of an essential human nature. Human individuals, we are told, think and act in accordance with the habits they have acquired, not in accordance with some inherent propensity towards rational behaviour or natural inclination to seek the true, the good, or the beautiful. Habits themselves are formed in response to repeated experiences of pleasure and pain, many of which will be occasioned by an individual's interactions with others. On this view we should treat our moral and aesthetic understandings and established patterns of conduct as the outcomes of habits of thought and of behaviour that are themselves the products of social conditioning. The formation of habit is the principal mechanism through which social arrangements, and especially the patterns of social interaction that take place within them, mould the thoughts and desires of individuals.

Locke's discussion also suggests what can be done to form the appropriate habits of thought and of behaviour in others, and indeed in oneself; or to change such habits as have already been formed. In other words, it provides the rationale for a variety of mechanisms, operating both directly and indirectly, that might be used in programs for the regulation of behaviour. At the simplest and most direct level, things should be so arranged that certain behaviours are rewarded and others penalized. In their endeavours to avoid pain, and to seek pleasure, people will normally learn to adopt the appropriate behaviour as a matter of course. Locke describes law as influencing behaviour in precisely this fashion.

But Locke's discussion also suggests that rewards and sanctions operate at a second, indirect level, and one that is in many respects more important. In addition to their direct effects on behaviour, rewards and sanctions can work to promote the habits of thought that govern what we agree to be true or false, good or evil: that is, they define the internal standards by which we each try to regulate our own judgements and behaviour. The significance of such internal standards is that they can be expected to operate in situations more or less remote from the conditions in which they were originally formed, and in particular in situations where external sanctioning mechanisms are either absent or ineffective. Behaviour may be regulated by the habits instilled through education, training and the appropriate disposition of reward and sanction, as well as by command and legal prohibition. On this account, education and the selective application of reward and sanction can be seen as a means of economizing on the direct use of sanctions. While the idea of sovereign power suggests that command and sanction are the principal means by which governments regulate the behaviour of their subjects, Locke's discussion suggests other, less direct modes of regulation.

What Locke presents in the *Essay* then is a model of the human individual as governed by acquired habits of thought and behaviour. He provides a straightforward account of the causes of those habits of thought and behaviour which might be regarded as undesirable: namely, that they are the result of poor education or bad company. The model also suggests a range of mechanisms that might be employed both in the direct regulation of behaviour and in the formation of individuals whose habits are such that they can normally be relied upon to regulate themselves. In other writings, Locke developed proposals for education and training, and for programs aimed at developing mental habits appropriate to the proper conduct of the understanding (Locke 1968). He also produced an influential report on reform of the poor law system which begins by lamenting the increasing numbers of the poor and the burden which their support imposes on the kingdom. There is, he suggests, no shortage of opportunities for employment, so the growth of the poor must have some other explanation:

and it can be nothing else but the relaxation of discipline and the corruption of manners; virtue and industry being as constant companions on the one side as vice and idleness are on the other. (Locke 1969, p. 378)

If the explanation for the growth of the poor lies in the development of bad habits, then the remedy is clear: break the bad habits and promote new ones in their place. 'The first step, therefore, towards the setting of the poor on work, we humbly conceive, ought to be a restraint of their debauchery by a strict execution of the laws provided against it. . . .' (ibid.). Locke's report goes on to propose a complex network of interrelated rewards and punishments designed to transform the system into a vast machine for reform and habituation.

This Lockean analysis of the role of acquired habits in the government of human behaviour is important here for two reasons. First, it shows how 'socially structured and culturally patterned behaviour' (Lukes 1974, p. 22) can affect the thoughts and desires of individuals. In this respect it provides one of the foundations of the 'radical' view of power that is the subject of this chapter. Secondly, it has been suggested (Tully 1989) that Locke was partly responsible for the construction of a new mode of governing conduct that came to the fore in Europe after the Reformation – although it is clear that closely related ideas concerning the indirect regulation of conduct by means of the formation of suitable habits were also being developed in other quarters.[1] We shall see in the next chapter that these and other mechanisms for the formation of self-regulating individuals are central components of the disciplinary and governmental powers which Foucault describes as characteristic of modern Western societies.

Civil Society

Neither republican doctrine nor the Lockean model of the individual as a creature of acquired habits is sufficient in itself to motivate Lukes' 'radical' view of power as a sinister and insidious force. Locke certainly proposes a variety of mechanisms whereby governments and other agencies can attempt to influence the thoughts and desires of individuals, but the use of those mechanisms can be readily assimilated to the conceptions of power considered in earlier chapters. It would not be difficult, for example, to interpret the uses of education, training and complex systems of reward and punishment to mould the capacities and attributes of individuals, either in terms of a republican conception of citizenship or as involving a straightforward generalization of the paternalistic rationale for the exercise of power. Even the misuse of such mechanisms could be seen, in Lockean terms, as a matter of tyranny or of usurpation. Nor is the idea of an insidious form of power required in order to make sense of numerous other cases where regimes of training and of rewards and punishments are regularly employed to mould behaviour, for example in prisons and in business enterprises. If these cases were to be conceptualized at all in terms of the operations of power, it would be of a power whose origins and presence would not be difficult to detect.

Lukes' conception of an insidious power acting on the thoughts and desires of individuals through the medium of social arrangements and patterns of behaviour involves a further element that has not yet been considered here. That is, it requires the idea of a power whose effects are produced in ways that cannot readily be traced to the deliberate actions of any identifiable individual or group.

In order to see how such a power might be expected to work, it is necessary to return first to the notion of civil society. I referred earlier to Koselleck's argument that, under the conditions of absolutist rule in much of Europe, Lockean ideas of government and of morality were likely to have been understood by the bourgeois intelligentsia as providing the foundations for a moral critique of political power (Koselleck 1988). Such a critique would have involved a conception of morality as a public force emerging from what later writers identified as 'civil society'; that is, from a realm of social interaction which is relatively free from direct state control.[2] Civil society, in this sense of the term, can be seen as regulating itself largely through the operations of Locke's 'Law of Opinion or Reputation'. The public morality that emerges from such operations appears to provide, at least in principle, the moral foundations on which the legitimacy of government should rest. These are also, of course, the same foundations on which a moral critique of political power might be developed. However, there is a further perspective on civil society that is relevant to the present discussion. Locke's account of the importance of habit in the regulation of thought and behaviour suggests that civil society should be seen not only as underlying a public morality, but also as an important source of our more private beliefs and desires.

Why should we think of this latter implication of Locke's 'Law of Opinion and Reputation' as relating to the exercise of power? In his careful analysis of contemporary theories of power, Wrong insists on the importance of distinguishing between power and social control:

> People exercise mutual influence and control over one another's conduct in all social interactions – in fact, that is what we mean by social interaction. It is essential, therefore, to distinguish between the exercise of power and social control in general – otherwise there would be no point in employing power as a separate concept or in identifying power relations as a distinct kind of social relation. (Wrong 1979, p. 3)

Lukes' claim that there is a form of power which works through 'socially structured and culturally patterned behaviour' (Lukes 1974, p. 22) suggests that much of what Wrong calls social control is more correctly described as the exercise – albeit insidious – of power.

In effect, Lukes' analysis requires that we regard many everyday social interactions as if they were instruments of power. What is involved here is a view of civil society both as a realm of social interaction and as an arena of contending social forces. To the extent that these forces can be regarded as representing the interests of particular social groups then, according to Lukes' account, the operations of Locke's 'Law of Opinion and Reputation' should be seen as an exercise of power serving the sectional interests of the strongest of these groups. On this view, it is only in the absence of such contending forces that civil society could be regarded simply as a realm of the interaction of free and equal citizens.

Marxism provides perhaps the most influential examples of this expanded conception of power through its accounts of civil society and the state as arenas of class struggle. While Marx admits that he adopted the notions of class and conflict between classes from the work of bourgeois historians, it is nevertheless Marxism that offers the most thoroughgoing elaboration of the notion of class conflict. Marxism maintains not only that the state serves the interests of the ruling class, but also that the structures of civil society itself will normally be dominated by that class. This means that for Marxists influential forms of morality and patterns of behaviour should be seen as serving the interests of the ruling class. The imagery of class struggle involves the idea that classes can themselves be considered as actors and therefore as agents capable of exercising power.[3] Marxism thus regards the ruling class as acting not only through the relatively direct and obvious instruments of state power, but also – and more insidiously – through the structures of civil society itself. In other words, what Wrong refers to simply as social control is taken to involve the exercise of power by the ruling class over all other classes.

It is a belief in the influence of particular social forces on civil society, and therefore on the thoughts and desires of individuals, that underlies Lukes' 'radical' view of power. In effect, Lukes presents us with a view of civil society as dominated both materially and 'ideally' by a powerful minority whose interests are opposed to the interests of the majority. The fact that the majority are prevented from recognizing their real interests ensures that they consent to their subordination. While such a view of power as operating in and through the life of civil society has been most clearly developed in Marxist thought, particularly in connection with the Gramscian notion of hegemony, it is not restricted to the analysis of society in terms of contending classes. Societies have also been analysed in terms of contending gender collectivities, leading to the idea of patriarchal power serving the interests of men by moulding the thoughts and desires of gendered persons through the institutions of politics and the economy, as well as through the patterns of daily life. Once civil society is conceived of as dominated in this way by powerful minority interests, then its members will be perceived as less than fully autonomous – and, in particular, as hardly fit to serve as citizens of the self-governing community posited by the argument of Locke's *Two Treatises of Government*. Neither the consent of such persons nor the morality that arises from their social interaction can suffice to legitimate political power.

Critical Theory and the 'radical' View of Power

I noted above that Locke could be seen as giving clear and forceful expression to two very different conceptions of the individual and therefore of the society to which

that individual belongs, both of which have since continued to play important parts in Western understandings
of political power. On the one hand, there is the idea of
the individual as possessed of inalienable rights and endowed with a faculty of reason. The assumption of a
community consisting of such individuals underlies the
logic of Locke's political argument in the *Two Treatises*
and gives that argument much of its rhetorical force.
On the other hand, there is the considerably more malleable individual who emerges from the pages of his
Essay. A community consisting of these latter individuals
would hardly constitute a self-governing political community of the kind posited by the argument of the *Two
Treatises* – unless, of course, they had already acquired
the appropriate   habits of thought and behaviour. This
is not the place to examine the many vicissitudes of these
conceptions, but it is worth noting two influential
strategies for dealing with the tensions between them.
One strategy involves recognizing, as Locke clearly does
in his *Second Treatise*, that people do not always behave
in accordance with the model of the free rational individual, while at the same time retaining that model as an
ideal, using it as the basis for a critique of the behaviour
of particular individuals or groups and even, rather more
generally, of the present organization of society. In effect, this strategy plays on both models of the individual,
treating each of them as representing an important, although partial, truth about society.

The second strategy is to treat neither of these conflicting conceptions of the individual as representing the
truth about society, but rather to treat each as an idea
that may be taken up in particular contexts of political
discussion. For those who adopt this strategy, what requires investigation are the contexts in which such ideas
are in fact employed and the consequences of their use in
those contexts. In contemporary discussions of power,

which particularly concern us here, the first strategy is most clearly represented in critical theory, and the second in some of the work of Foucault and his associates. I shall comment briefly on critical theory below, and turn to Foucault in the following chapter.

The first of these strategies makes use of the normative ideal of a community of autonomous persons to create a measure of the impact of power. Lukes' 'radical view' of power is a good example of such an argument. He describes his third dimension of power as operating to prevent individuals from recognizing their real interests. Thus person A may exercise power over person B, not only by getting B to do what she would prefer not to do, but also by influencing what she would prefer to do by preventing her from recognizing her own real interests. 'The identification of these [interests]' Lukes tells us 'is not up to A, but to B, exercising choice under conditions of relative autonomy and, in particular, independently of A's power – e.g. through democratic participation' (Lukes 1974, p. 33). Here the true workings of power are to be revealed through invocation of the imaginary ideals first of individual autonomy and secondly of the kind of civil society in which such autonomy could be found. The truth that Lukes' radical view of power allows him to uncover is simply the difference between the ideal and the mundane; that is, between Locke's two contrasting models of the human individual. Those who do not fully share the ideal – or who see the alternative Lockean model as 'the truth' – will be unable to perceive the truth which that ideal is able to reveal. Conversely, those who cannot see that 'truth' must be regarded by those who can, either as opponents of the ideal of autonomy or as unfortunate victims of the power of those opponents.

Lukes' short book presents us with an account of the 'radical view' of power promised by its subtitle that is forceful, but also rather schematic. More fully elaborated versions of this view of power have been developed by critical theory, which combines a modified Enlightenment view of reason with a psychoanalytic account of the individual on the one hand, and a Marxist analysis of society on the other. Let me conclude this chapter, by way of illustration, with some brief comments on the conceptualization of power in Marcuse's *One Dimensional Man* (1972) and in the later work of Habermas. There can be no question here of attempting to provide a full account of the work of these authors. My comments are intended merely to demonstrate the use in their arguments of the view of power sketched above, and in particular their use of the strategy set out at the beginning of this section, in which an imaginary ideal is invoked in order to reveal what is thought to be the truth of modern society.

In *One Dimensional Man*, Marcuse claims that advanced industrial societies have made liberty 'into a powerful instrument of domination' (Marcuse 1972, p. 21). In other words, the 'free' choices made by individual members of those societies serve to perpetuate a set of power relations that further the interests of those who dominate. What makes it possible for 'free' decisions to have this effect is that the system of domination itself provides its victims with misleading understandings of their real interests. Consequently, Marcuse insists:

> The fact that the vast majority of the population accepts, and is made to accept, this society does not render it less irrational and less reprehensible. (ibid., p. 12)

In fact, we are told, false needs have been 'superimposed' on individuals by 'external powers' over which they have no control: 'the development and satisfaction of these needs is heteronomous' (ibid., p. 19). We act freely, in

Marcuse's view, on the basis of thoughts and desires that have been imposed on us from without, most obviously perhaps through propaganda and manipulation carried by the media. Marcuse nevertheless insists that the direct impact of the media should not be overrated. People entering the stage of manipulation by the media are already 'preconditioned receptacles of long standing' (ibid., p. 21). In fact, he argues, 'massive socialisation begins at home' (ibid., p. 192). At one time, Marcuse believes, the family provided a space for the formation of 'an individual consciousness and an individual unconscious *apart* from public opinion and behaviour' (ibid., p. 22), but many of its socializing functions have now been taken over by outside groups and by the media (cf. Marcuse 1955). The result is that what had once, in his view, been a 'private space in which man may become and remain "himself" ' . . . has been invaded and whittled down by technological reality' (ibid., pp. 22–3). The individual no longer has the inner resources to stand against the demands of society.

Marcuse's analysis of domination contains all the ingredients noted above of the 'radical' view of power as working on the thoughts and desires of individuals through the medium of social conditions – to which he adds a psychoanalytic account of personality formation. First, there is the view that individual behaviour in advanced industrial societies is governed by acquired habits which are themselves seen as products of interaction with our peers, the media and the helping professions. In principle, Marcuse suggests, it should be possible for individuals to resist the impact of such forces, but in these societies the family environment which might be expected to foster the development of suitably robust personalities has itself been undermined by external social forces. Secondly, Marcuse invokes the image of individual autonomy as providing an ideal against which the present can be measured. It is precisely because advanced industrial societies and families within them are dominated by class and other forces that they provide little scope for real autonomy. Finally, Marcuse suggests a view of conditions under which the ideal of individual autonomy could be realized. These conditions bring together at one level a sphere of family and private life that promotes the formation of autonomous personalities and, at another level, a civil society that is no longer structured by oppressive social forces. The ideal can be realized, then, only to the extent that

> the masses have been dissolved into individuals liberated from all propaganda, indoctrination, and manipulation, capable of knowing and comprehending the facts and of evaluating the alternatives. (ibid., p. 196)

In the earlier critical tradition the operation of the 'Law of Opinion and Reputation' was thought to provide foundations for an independent moral critique of political power. The Marxist analysis of civil society as itself structured by class forces suggested that any such moral critique would in fact be far from independent of the interests of the ruling class. Even under such conditions, Marcuse suggests, the family and private life had once been able to provide a space in which an independent moral standpoint could be developed. In the modern world, however, that limited sphere of autonomy has itself been largely taken over by external forces. In Marcuse's view, then, society no longer provides a place from which an independent moral critique of existing social conditions could be elaborated. He is therefore led to the conclusion that the only hope for the development of a rational society of autonomous individuals lies with 'the outcasts and outsiders', that is, with those who have not been granted the benefits of incorporation into the overall system of domination.

One Dimensional Man is the most pessimistic of Marcuse's works, and its conclusion reflects a deeper concern with the character of enlightenment itself. In effect, the Frankfurt School theorists share many of Weber's reservations about the consequences of rationalization, treating it as resulting at one level in a loss of meaning and at another level in the subordination of the individual to the requirements of bureaucracy. Their commitment to enlightenment and to reason is therefore highly ambivalent. In that respect there are significant parallels between the later work of the Frankfurt School and the arguments of Foucault, Derrida and other 'post-modernists'.

This point brings us to Habermas's elaboration and development of the critical theory tradition. His earliest major work, only recently translated into English (Habermas 1989), is a study of the emergence and development of a public sphere (that is, civil society) in the seventeenth and eighteenth centuries, and of its later distortion and disintegration. This study may be regarded as elaborating on some of the central concerns of the earlier generation of critical theorists, but Habermas has since become increasingly critical of that earlier generation's treatment of rationality. His attempts to provide the critical project with more secure intellectual foundations have gone through several stages, culminating in his two-volume work *The Theory of Communicative Action* (Habermas 1984, 1987). In his view, the major figures of the earlier generation were too prone to treat questions concerning the conditions of reason and of knowledge as if they were about the situation of the individual subject. They therefore paid insufficient attention to the intersubjective conditions of rationality and of the formation of the individual in the course of interaction with others. Negative features which they attributed to rationalization should rather, in Habermas's opinion, be seen as consequences of the social conditions in which rationalization has taken place.

Certainly, compared with Marcuse's bleak polemic, the later work of Habermas provides an account of modern society that is considerably more complex and, in many respects, more sophisticated. Nevertheless, his analysis of modern society remains crucially dependent on the 'radical' view of power outlined above. Two features of Habermas's argument are particularly important in this connection. First, Habermas regards the earlier generation of critical theorists as limited by their commitment to a 'philosophy of the subject' (Habermas 1984, especially ch. 4). In its place he proposes a philosophy of intersubjectivity, making use of Mead's interactionism, phenomenological sociology and linguistic philosophy.[4] Secondly, his account of how society is itself structured by social forces makes considerable use of contemporary non-Marxist social theory.

His stress on intersubjectivity enables Habermas to propose a theory of rationality in which the central concern is not so much with the role of the individual subject as it is with the individual as member of a lifeworld that is shared with other individuals and collectivities. On this view, the scope for individual rationality and autonomy will depend on the character of the lifeworld of which the individual is a part – just as, in Locke's analysis, the rationality or otherwise of the individual will depend in large part on the habits of thought and behaviour promoted by the operations of the law of opinion and reputation. Language and intersubjective relations are central to Habermas's analysis of the lifeworld. In particular, he insists 'that the use of language with an orientation to reaching understanding is the *original mode* of language use' (Habermas 1984, p. 288). Instrumental and other uses of language are parasitic on that original mode.

Habermas maintains that the intrusion of power into intersubjective relations will distort the original orientation towards understanding, thereby undermining the rationality of both the lifeworld and its individual inhabitants.

In Habermas's view, however, the rationality of the lifeworld and of individuals within it requires more than the simple absence of domination. Habermas takes over some of Weber's concerns with the distinctive rationality of the West in contrast to the world views he sees as characterizing other societies. This suggests that, even without the distorting impact of power, the rationality of the lifeworld cannot be taken for granted. Accordingly he proposes an account of the rationalization of the lifeworld as a specific historical process (Habermas 1984, p. 43f.). What distinguishes a rationalized lifeworld from one still dominated by tradition is that in the former

> the need for achieving understanding is met less and less by a reservoir of traditionally certified interpretations immune from criticism; [rather it is met] more and more frequently by risky, because rationally motivated, agreement. (ibid., p. 340)

Only in such a rationalized lifeworld, Habermas suggests, should we expect to find rational, autonomous individuals. However, like the earlier Frankfurt generation, he recognizes that we rarely find such individuals even in the rationalized societies of the modern West. As a measure of the limited rationality of these societies, Habermas introduces the notion of an ideal speech situation. It refers to a condition of uncoerced discussion between free and equal individuals in which, Habermas maintains, communication will be organized around the attempt to reach rationally motivated agreement (Habermas 1973, pp. 211f., 1990, pp. 88f.). However, the intrusion into the lifeworld of power or coercion leads to communication that is structured around other concerns, resulting at best in agreement, or rather the appearance of agreement, arising from fear, deference, insecurity and other such non-rational motivations. In this respect, the effect of power is to undermine the rationality even of a rationalized lifeworld.

A distinct, but related, aspect of the rationalization of the lifeworld, in Habermas's view, is that it leads to the emergence of a 'political public sphere of private persons ... which, as a medium for permanent criticism, alters the conditions for the legitimation of political domination' (Habermas 1984, p. 341). Here Habermas invokes both the image of a political community of autonomous citizens, which plays a fundamental role in the argument of Locke's *Second Treatise*, and the idea that their everyday interaction provides the moral foundations for a critique of political power. In effect, Habermas's political public sphere corresponds to the idea of an autonomous civil society noted earlier. Whether the political public sphere will perform that function in practice depends on the extent to which the conditions of discussion remain undistorted by the effects of power.

As for Habermas's use of non-Marxist social theory in analysing how society itself is structured, I have already noted his reworking of the Weberian theme of rationalization, but his adaptation of the systems theories of Parsons and Niklas Luhman is equally significant. In effect, Habermas suggests that we should analyse society from both a lifeworld and a systems perspective. This enables him to rework what he sees as the Weberian paradox, according to which the process of rationalization involves both a loss of meaning and a development leading to a significant loss of freedom. Where Weber and the earlier Frankfurt School theorists saw these and many other negative features of the modern West as arising from the process of rationalization itself, Habermas insists that they should count as effects of the 'uncoupling of system and lifeworld' (Habermas 1987, p. 318). Habermas argues both that rationalization provided the conditions in which societal media,[5] especially power and money, could emerge, and that these media have subsequently worked 'back upon contexts of communicative action and set their own imperatives against the marginalised lifeworld' (ibid.). Fortunately, the details of this process need not concern us here. What matters for the present discussion is that what Weber and the earlier Frankfurt School theorists had seen as the negative effects of rationalization can be described by Habermas as 'pathological variants' in which 'the mediatization of the lifeworld turns into its colonization' (ibid.). The term 'pathological' here suggests that it may be possible to develop 'non-pathological' variants in which the lifeworld remains undistorted either by the intrusion of societal media or by other effects of power and coercion.

For all his criticism of the earlier generation of critical theorists, then, Habermas retains much of its critical orientation. First, human individuals are presented as creatures of their lifeworld – much as the individuals of Locke's *Essay* are presented as creatures of the conditions in which they interact with others. Secondly, the image of a rationalized lifeworld that is oriented to the requirements of an ideal speech situation (and therefore to individual autonomy) serves as a standpoint from which the present organization of society can be judged and found to be pathological. However, in addition to its normative use, this idealized condition is also employed by Habermas in a descriptive sense to provide a measure of the distorting impact of power (and money) on what would otherwise be a rationally ordered lifeworld. As with Marcuse's argument, then, the real impact of power (and of money) in Habermas's account is to be identified by reference to society's failure to measure up to an imaginary ideal in which individuals can interact on an undistorted and autonomous basis.

In spite of their many differences, Lukes, Marcuse and Habermas all base a significant part of their analyses of power on: (1) a model of the individual as a creature of social conditions; (2) an image of the autonomous individual which provides an ideal against which the present can be measured; (3) the claim that such an ideal could be realized in a realm of social existence that is not structured by the illegitimate effects of power. This last presents us with the utopian vision of an idealized civil society whose inhabitants would be precisely the autonomous, rational persons required by the Lockean account of political power. In their different ways, then, all three acknowledge the reality of heteronomy – the fact that the attributes and capacities of persons are crucially dependent on social conditions – while retaining the Lockean ideal of the autonomous, rational person. The invocation, first of these distinct conceptions of the human individual and, secondly, of a view of civil society as an arena of contending social forces, is the core of the 'radical' view of power.

5

discipline and cherish:
Foucault on Power, Domination and Government

The authors considered in my earlier chapters regard power as enhancing the capacities of those who possess it and consequently, in so far as it impinges on other persons, as an imposition on the freedom of those persons. In this latter aspect, the effects of power are most commonly identified by reference to counterfactual conditions: power in the hands of others prevents its victims from doing what they otherwise would have done, from obtaining what they otherwise would have obtained, or even from thinking what they otherwise would have thought. With regard to political power, in particular, the most influential traditions of modern political thought have been especially concerned with questions of sovereignty and of legitimacy, and they have identified the most significant effects of political power with reference to the condition of those who are regarded, at least in principle, as autonomous moral agents. As a result, the imposition of power is seen as legitimate if it is based on the real or implied consent of such persons. All other impositions are seen either as illegitimate or, at best, as bearing on persons who are regarded as less than fully autonomous and therefore as being without the capacity either to give their consent or to withhold it. In the case of critical theory, and to some extent more generally, a particular kind of illegitimate power is identified as one of the most important obstacles to the achievement of individual autonomy.

I now turn to the work of Foucault, which is important here precisely because he insists that the study of power needs to move away from these obsessions with questions of sovereignty and legitimacy. 'We need', he tells us, 'to cut off the King's head: in political theory that has still to be done' (Foucault 1980, p. 121). This chapter outlines Foucault's analysis of power, and of governmental power in particular, and considers how it differs from the analyses of political power considered in my earlier chapters. I begin by discussing Foucault's distinctions between, on the one hand, power in general and, on the other, domination and government. Foucault conceives of power in terms of a 'structure of actions' (ibid., p. 220) bearing on the actions of those who are free. It follows from this, in his view, that power relationships will often be unstable and reversible. His conceptions of domination and government, however, are intended to designate power relationships that are relatively stable and hierarchical. Domination refers to conditions under which the subordinated have relatively little room for manoeuvre. Government lies between domination and those relationships of power which are reversible; it is the conduct of conduct, aiming to affect the actions of individuals by working on their conduct – that is, on the ways in which they regulate their own behaviour.

The greater part of this chapter is devoted to Foucault's discussions of government as it has emerged in the societies of the modern West. His account can be seen as presenting a clear alternative to the conceptualization, considered in my earlier chapters, of power as if it is, or should be, a function of consent. Rather than exploring questions to do with the legitimacy of governmental power, Foucault is concerned to understand the means whereby the effects of such power are produced. He focuses, therefore, on the techniques of government and, especially, on its *rationalities*; that is, on discourses that address practical questions concerning how to conduct the conduct of the state and of the population which the state claims to rule. From this perspective, the notion of a sovereign (or political) power that rules on the basis of consent can be seen as implicated in simply one among a number of influential rationalities of government, and therefore needing to be accorded no special analytical privilege. In view of the attention given to such an idea of power in chapters 2, 3 and 4 above, I concentrate here on Foucault's treatment of three other rationalities of government which he regards as having been particularly influential in the development of the modern West: discipline, the 'shepherd–flock game', and liberalism. My concluding chapter considers some of the limitations of Foucault's approach and, in particular, takes up the question of whether he himself manages to escape the problems and presumptions which he is concerned to critique.

Power and Domination

One of the problems with discussing Foucault's treatment of power is that there seems to have been a substantial change in his usage of the term in the period immediately following his examination of the disciplines in *Discipline and Punish* (1979a) and his treatment of biopolitics in volume 1 of *The History of Sexuality* (1979b). According to Pasquino, who worked closely with Foucault at this time, Foucault appears to have realized that his earlier treatment of power had 'threatened to lead to an extremist denunciation of power – envisaged according to a repressive model' (Pasquino

1992, p. 79). In its place, Pasquino suggests, Foucault began to address the 'question of *government* – a term that Foucault gradually substituted for what he began to see as the more ambiguous word, "power" ' (ibid.; cf. Foucault 1988a, p. 19). It is this later, less denunciatory, understanding of power, and especially of government, that is of most interest here. My earlier chapters have suggested that much of the discussion of power in Western political thought has been animated by broader concerns with the political constitution of society and, especially, with relations between government and its citizens. Foucault's treatment of government as a distinctive modality of the exercise of power brings us back to those concerns, albeit from a rather different angle.

In one of his final interviews Foucault insists that:

> we must distinguish the relationships of power as strategic games between liberties – strategic games that result in the fact that some people try to determine the conduct of others – and the states of domination, which are what we ordinarily call power. And, between the two, between the games of power and the states of domination, you have governmental technologies . . . (1988a, p. 19)

Three types of power relationship are identified in this extract: strategic games between liberties, domination and government. I consider the first and second of these in this section and move on to the third in the section that follows.

The reference to 'power as strategic games between liberties' suggests that in Foucault's view there is an intimate relationship between power and liberty. This is, in fact, the core of Foucault's understanding of power in general. Power, as Foucault presents it, is 'the total structure of actions' (Foucault 1980, p. 220) bearing on the actions of individuals who are free; that is, whose own behaviour is not wholly determined by physical constraints. Power is exercised over those who are in a position to choose, and it aims to influence what their choices will be. I noted in chapter 2 that Hobbes' definition of power refers to a heterogeneous collection of attributes and possessions with nothing in common apart from the fact that they might prove useful to their possessors. A similar point can be made for Foucault's rather different understanding of power as a structure of actions. Power, in this sense, is manifested in the instruments, techniques and procedures that may be brought to bear on the actions of others. This, too, suggests that the forms of power may be remarkably heterogeneous, and that some will be concentrated and hierarchically organized while others will be socially dispersed.

On this view, power – and the resistance and evasion that it provokes – must be regarded as a ubiquitous feature of human interaction. Power is everywhere and it is available to anyone. It may be deployed in pursuit of any objective and its uses may be analysed in terms of the most varied instrumental and evaluative considerations. Such banalities apart, this account of power appears to suggest that there is little of value to be said about power in general. Indeed, there are passages in Foucault's work which express a profound scepticism about the utility of the notion. In 'The subject and power', for example, Foucault comments that to ask 'How do things happen?'

> is to suggest that power as such does not exist. At the very least it is to ask what contents one has in mind when using this all-embracing and reifying term: it is to suspect that an extremely complex configuration of realities is allowed to escape when one treads endlessly the double question: What is power?

and Where does power come from? (Foucault 1982,
p. 217)

To insist, as Foucault does, that the exercise of power
requires a degree of freedom on the part of its subjects is
to say, first, that the effective exercise of power need not
imply the removal of liberty. On the contrary, in Foucault's view, where there is no possibility of resistance
there can be no relations of power. It follows that the
exercise of power will normally be at risk from the recalcitrance of its subjects: it will always involve costs and its
outcome will often be far from certain. Resistance, evasion
and the costs of dealing with them may provoke refinement or modification of the techniques of power – and
these, in turn, will provide conditions under which new
forms of resistance and evasion may be developed. In
Foucault's view, then, the study of power is certainly not
the study of a quantitative capacity or essence of effectiveness of the kind that the mechanical view examined in
chapter 2 appears to require. Rather, he suggests that it
should be the study of 'the total structure of actions
brought to bear' (Foucault 1982, p. 220) on the actions of
others in particular cases, and of the resistances and evas-
ions encountered by those actions.

To say that those who are subject to the effects of
power are free is to say, secondly, that they are themselves in a position to act on the actions of others; that is,
to engage in the exercise of power on their own account.
For this reason, in Foucault's view, relationships of
power will often be unstable, ambiguous and reversible.
In such cases the exercise of power will indeed be a
matter of 'strategic games between liberties'. Foucault
illustrates this reversibility of power by reference to the
ways in which the fact

that I am older and that at first you were intimidated

> can, in the course of the conversation, turn about
> and it is I who can become intimidated before some-
> one, precisely because he is younger. (Foucault
> 1988a, p. 12)

Relationships of power that can be reversed in this way
are not unlike those somewhat idealized relationships
between citizens described in Aristotle's *Politics* (1988,
p. 17), who rule and are ruled by turns. Again, Foucault's
account differs markedly, in this respect, from the conception of power as simple capacity considered in the
first part of chapter 2. While the latter seems to suggest
that those with more power will invariably prevail over
those with less, Foucault eschews any such merely quantitative understanding of the differences between one
power and another.

  We shall see that Foucault has a marked preference for
relationships of power that are reversible. However, he
clearly recognizes that relationships of power often have
a very different structure. Towards the beginning of this
section, I quoted Foucault's use of the term 'domination'
to designate 'what we ordinarily call power'. Domination
refers, in other words, to those asymmetrical relationships
of power in which the subordinated persons have little
room for manoeuvre because their 'margin of liberty is
extremely limited' (Foucault 1988a, p. 12) by the effects of
power. In these relationships, those who dominate have a
good chance of being able to impose their will, even, as
Weber puts it, 'against the resistance of others who are
participating in the action' (Weber 1978, p. 926). Domination, in other words, is a particular modality of the
exercise of power. Even here, however, Foucault insists
that the situation is never entirely one-sided:

> Even though the relation of power may be complete-
> ly unbalanced or when one can truly say that he has

'all power' over the other, a power can only be exercised over another to the extent that the latter still
has the possibility of committing suicide, of jumping
out of the window or of killing the other. (Foucault
1988a, p. 12)

power is reversable

What Foucault came to see as problematic in his earlier
discussions of power is largely a consequence of the fact
that they make no clear distinction between power relationships in general and domination as a particular type
of power relationship that is both stable and hierarchical.
Since Foucault has always presented power as an ubiquitous feature of human interaction, much of what he has
to say on the topic can thus be read as suggesting that
hierarchical relationships of power are inescapable. Indeed, precisely that view is forcefully expressed in Foucault's Nietzschean account of history as an 'endlessly
repeated play of domination' (Foucault 1977, p. 150).[1]
Each domination

is fixed, throughout its history, in rituals, in meticulous procedures that impose rights and obligations
. . . . the law is a calculated and relentless pleasure,
delight in the promised blood, which permits the
perpetual instigation of new dominations and the
staging of meticulously repeated scenes of violence
. . . . Humanity does not gradually progress from
combat to combat until it finally arrives at universal
reciprocity, where the rule of law finally replaces
warfare; humanity installs each of its violences in a
system of rules and thus proceeds from domination
to domination. (Foucault 1977, pp. 150–1)

Why should this elision of power and domination be
seen, in Pasquino's words, as tending towards 'an extremist denunciation of power' (Pasquino 1992, p. 79)?

The answer is that in much of Foucault's work, as in much of critical theory, domination is regarded as something that should be avoided whenever possible. This means that domination must be distinguished from power in general if the latter is not to be seen as bad in itself. Once such a distinction is made, the problem becomes one not of the avoiding or minimizing relationships of power, but, rather, one of establishing conditions 'which would allow these games of power to be played with a minimum of domination' (Foucault 1988a, p. 18). Just as Lukes and the Frankfurt School condemn certain kinds of power in the name of an ideal of individual autonomy, so there are passages in Foucault's later work on power in which he appears to condemn domination in the name of liberty. The dream of 'universal reciprocity', so contemptuously dismissed in the extract from 'Nietzsche, Genealogy, History' quoted above, is presented in these passages almost as if it could be seen as a regulative ideal. In fact, Foucault goes on to insist that the critical function of philosophy

> is precisely the challenging of all phenomena of domination at whatever level or under whatever form they present themselves – political, economic, sexual, institutional, and so on. This critical function . . . emerges right from the Socratic imperative: 'Be concerned with yourself, i.e., ground yourself in liberty, through the mastery of self'. (Foucault, 1988a, p. 20)

An important consequence of Foucault's distinction between power and domination, then, is that it allows him to condemn states of domination in contrast to 'strategic games of power between liberties'. I will return, in chapter 6, to consider this and other parallels between Foucault's treatment of domination and the 'radical' view of power discussed in chapter 4.

Government

The third of Foucault's types of power relationship is government, and his discussions of this can be seen as presenting a clear alternative to analyses of political power in terms of the questions of sovereignty and legitimacy considered in my earlier chapters. Immediately following his insistence on the differences between games of power, domination and government in the interview cited earlier, Foucault goes on to say that we should give this last term 'a very wide meaning, for it is also the way in which you govern your wife, your children, as well as the way you govern an institution' (Foucault 1988a, p. 19). Here, and in his 'Governmentality' lecture (Foucault 1991), Foucault maintains that, in spite of the different specific objectives and fields to which the term is applied, there is a certain continuity between the government of oneself, the government of a household and the government of a state or community. Linked to this continuity, he argues, is the fact that the principles of political action and those of personal conduct can be seen as being intimately related. He suggests, for example, that successful government of others depends, in the first instance, on the capacity of those doing the governing to govern themselves. As for the governed, to the extent that it avoids the extremes of domination, their government must aim to affect their *conduct* – that is, it must operate through their capacity to regulate their own behaviour. In this respect too, successful *government* of others is often thought to depend on the ability of those others to govern themselves, and it must therefore aim to secure the conditions under which they are enabled to do so.

However, and in spite of the continuity that he discerns between the different usages of the term 'government', the greater part of Foucault's published work in the period following his reconsideration of power takes the form of a genealogy of ethics. It focuses, in other words, on questions of the government of oneself, considering the government of others largely only in so far as this bears on that more central concern. Foucault examined the government of others at length in a series of lectures at the Collège de France in 1978 and 1979 but, with the exception of the 'Governmentality' lecture (Foucault 1991), these remain unpublished. Otherwise, his analysis of government of the state must be pieced together from the ideas sketched out in a few short, and sometimes enigmatic, essays and interviews.[2]

In his 'Governmentality' lecture, and in many of his later lectures and interviews, the term 'government' is particularly associated with notions of 'conducting' (in the sense of leading or controlling a series of actions), of 'rationality' and of 'technology'. 'Government' refers, in other words, to certain less spontaneous exercises of power over others (to those exercises that are more calculated and considered) and, particularly, to the use and invention of technologies for the regulation of conduct. It refers, then, to the regulation of conduct through the more or less rational application of the appropriate technical means. A closely related point is that government, as Foucault describes it, aims to regulate the *conduct* of others or of oneself. In addition to acting directly on individual behaviour, it thus aims to affect behaviour indirectly by acting on the manner in which individuals regulate their own behaviour. In this respect, too, government involves an element of calculation – and a knowledge of its intended object – that is not necessarily present in every exercise of power.

Government, in this sense, is something which one

would expect to find in most, if not all, human societies. Foucault's assertion that we 'live in the era of a "governmentality" first discovered in the eighteenth century' (Foucault 1991, p. 91) should not be understood as meaning that the idea of government was itself something of a novelty at that time. His point rather is that there has developed a certain kind of reflection on government (which I consider below). He also suggests that there has been an expansion of government itself relative to straightforward domination on the one hand and to unstable and reversible relations of power on the other.

In fact, Foucault suggests that certain questions concerning government emerged with particular force in parts of sixteenth-century Europe: what does governing consist in? which persons or institutions can govern? who or what is governed or is capable of being governed? He argues that these questions arose largely as a consequence of two developments. First, there was the breakdown of feudal institutions and the formation of territorial, administrative states. One important consequence of the weakening of feudal ties was that matters of individual conduct could no longer be regarded as regulated effectively by networks of personal dependence and reciprocal obligation. Questions of the government of oneself, and of who could legitimately claim to govern that government, therefore assumed a particular significance at a time when the newly emerging states were attempting to establish their own systems of large-scale administration. The emergence of the state as an identifiable institutional structure distinct from the person or persons of the ruler suggested, at least in principle, that questions concerning government of, and by, the state could be separated from questions concerning the personal power or security of the ruler. The second development was the spread of the Reformation and Counter-Reformation, which raised disputes over spiritual rule to the level of conflicts between and within states. On the one hand, this development resulted in the formation of distinct Catholic, Lutheran and Calvinist states, in each of which techniques and rationalities of spiritual rule were taken up in the service of state administrations.[3] On the other hand, the common problems faced by the diverse 'confessional' states fostered the idea that the state had properties and objectives of its own, that is, properties and objectives of a kind that did not depend on disputed theological justifications. As a consequence of these two developments, it became possible to maintain that there was a distinctive 'reason of state', reducible neither to religion nor to a concern with the power or security of the sovereign.

While in his lectures on governmental rationality Foucault focuses largely on the political domain – that is, on issues pertaining to the government of a state or community – he conducts his analysis largely in terms of the primary sense of government as the regulation of conduct through the more or less rational application of the appropriate technical means. It is in this sense, for example, that he is able to refer to 'the governmentalization of the state' (Foucault 1991, p. 103). By this he means, first, that the activities of the state have increasingly taken the form of *government* – that is, of attending to the *conduct* of its subjects as distinct from relying on *ad hoc* interventions, law- enforcement and straightforward domination – and, secondly, that the state itself has been subsumed as a set of instruments within broader programs of government:

> it is the tactics of government which make possible the continual definition and redefinition of what is within the competence of the state and what is not, the public versus the private, and so on. (ibid.)

From this point of view, what matters in the study of governmental power is not so much the state itself, considered as a more or less unified set of instrumentalities, but rather the broader strategies of government within which the instrumentalities of the state are incorporated and deployed. I return to the significance of this point shortly.

However, Foucault also acknowledges a second, more specific usage of the term 'government': one which relates more directly to the conceptions of political power considered in my earlier chapters. Thus he notes that

> among all these forms of government which interweave within the state and society, there remains one special and precise form: there is the question of defining the particular form of governing which can be applied to the state as a whole. (Foucault 1991, p. 91)

In referring to this 'special and precise form' of government, Foucault aims to distinguish government of, and through, the state both from government of oneself or of one's household, and from the form of rule to be found in the societies of late feudal Europe or of classical antiquity. Government, in this specific sense, is not to be confused with the rule of the prince, feudal magnate or emperor, or even with the collective rule over themselves and others that is often said to have been exercised by citizens of the independent Greek communities and of the Roman republic.

No doubt much of what is at issue in such differences is already covered by the suggestion, noted above, that what particularly distinguishes government from other forms of power is the element of rational calculation. But a further important element appears in Foucault's contrast between the early modern understanding of the art of government and what he calls the problematic of the prince – that is, the concept of rule so clearly set out in Machiavelli's text of that name (written in 1513). Where the problematic of the prince is concerned with 'the prince's ability to keep his principality', Foucault tells us that the anti-Machiavellian literature of the following two centuries wishes to replace this concern with 'something else and new, namely the *art of government*' (Foucault 1991, p. 90; emphasis added). He notes that this new

> art of government finds its first form of crystallisation, organised around the theme of reason of state, understood not in the negative and pejorative sense we give to it today . . . but in a full and positive sense: *the state is governed according to rational principles which are intrinsic to it* and which cannot be derived solely from natural or divine laws or the principles of wisdom and prudence. (ibid., pp. 96–7; emphasis added)

We shall see shortly that there is more to Foucault's account of the art of government than its elaboration around the theme of reason of state. Nevertheless, this last extract highlights an essential feature of Foucault's second, more specific, usage of the term 'government'. What distinguishes the idea of the art of government from other conceptions of political rule, in Foucault's view, is its association with the idea of the state in something like its modern form; in other words, with the idea of the state as referring, first, to a distinctive institutional structure that can be seen as existing independently of the prince or any other holder of sovereign power and, secondly, to the population that is ruled by such an institutional structure.

   In this more specific usage, it might seem that modern

political theory's identification of government with the activities of the state (that is, of *the* government) is particularly apposite. However, Foucault's argument serves to undermine that view. He goes on to insist that the association of the art of government with 'this form of "reason of state" acted as a sort of obstacle to the development of the art of government' (Foucault 1991, p. 97). This obstacle has several causes, but among the most important, in Foucault's view, is the fact that 'reason of state' is primarily concerned with the exercise of sovereignty – that is, with the interests of 'the state' in the first and narrower sense just noted. I suggested in chapter 3 that the view of sovereign power as founded on consent does provide a limited answer to the problem of how to conduct the conduct of others, but that it does so only because the slippage between the ideas of power as a right and power as a capacity allows the answer to the question of legitimacy to appear as if it is also an answer to the practical problem of government.

What ultimately enabled the art of government to develop independently of the problem of sovereignty, according to Foucault, is the emergence of an understanding of the domain of population as having 'its own regularities, its own rate of deaths and diseases, its cycles of scarcity, etc' (Foucault 1991, p. 99), that is, as characterized by its own aggregate phenomena, irreducible to those of the families contained within it. There are two distinct but related issues here. First, Foucault suggests that this understanding of population displaces the family from its preeminent position as a model for government: now it is viewed simply as a segment of the population that has to be governed. Secondly, he argues that population

comes to appear above all else as the ultimate end of government. In contrast to sovereignty, government

> has as its purpose not the act of government itself,
> but the welfare of the population, the improvement
> of its condition, the increase of its wealth, longevity,
> health, etc.; and the means that the government uses
> to attain those ends are themselves all in some sense
> immanent to the population. (ibid., p. 100)

Government, in other words, is concerned with managing the population of the state and the institutions, organizations and processes which that population encompasses. From this standpoint, the agencies of the state appear as one, albeit significant, set of instruments of government amongst others, and as part of the population that is to be governed. It is for this reason that Foucault insists, in the passage quoted above, that it is not so much the state, considered as a distinctive institutional structure, that determines 'what is within the competence of the state and what is not, the public and the private, and so on' (Foucault 1991, p. 91). Rather, this is determined by specific rationalities of government.

Once the question of government is distinguished from that of sovereignty in this way, consideration of the practical art or rationality of government must be distinguished from consideration of the normative basis of sovereignty. While, as we have seen, the theory of sovereignty can provide a limited answer to the general problem of government, Foucault argues that other approaches to conceptualizing the government of others have also been influential in the history of the modern West, even if they have not always been canonized in what we now tend to think of as the classics of modern social and political thought. He pays particular attention to three such approaches to the general problem of government: discipline, pastoral power and liberalism.[4] The greater part of this chapter is devoted to outlining what he has to say about each of these perspectives. My aim here is not to endorse his analysis, but rather to clarify what is at stake for political theory in the Foucauldian understanding of government. A brief concluding section considers the implications of this analysis of government for the broad understanding of political power set out in my first few chapters.

Discipline

In *Discipline and Punish* (Foucault 1979a, especially Part Three) Foucault describes discipline as a specific form of power, emerging in seventeenth-century Europe and continuing throughout the history of the modern West. It is a power exercised over one or more individuals in order to provide them with particular skills and attributes, to develop their capacity for self-control, to promote their ability to act in concert, to render them amenable to instruction, or to mould their characters in other ways. While discipline frequently involves repression, Foucault insists that it should not be seen as being essentially repressive or negative in character. In his view, discipline is a productive power *par excellence*: it aims not only to constrain those over whom it is exercised, but also to enhance and make use of their capacities.

I noted earlier that Foucault developed his distinctions between power, domination and government only after he had completed his work on the disciplines. Nevertheless, it is clear that much of what he has to say about discipline should be located within the framework of his later discussions of government. For example, in his 'Governmentality' lecture, Foucault notes that discipline's

modes of organisation, all the institutions within which it had developed in the seventeenth and eighteenth centuries – schools, manufactories, armies,

etc. – all this can only be understood on the basis of
the development of the great administrative mon-
archies . . . (Foucault 1991, pp. 101–2)

In fact, *Discipline and Punish* documents not so much
the presence of disciplinary techniques (which has been a
feature of most, if not all, human communities), but
rather the proliferation in seventeenth-century Europe of
proposals to use such techniques for a variety of practical
purposes: education and training, military organization,
the regulation of hospitals, prisons and other institutions
of confinement, and so on. Foucault writes of the proliferation of disciplinary proposals at this time as if discipline had now begun to be seen as a generalized means of
controlling and making use of human behaviour, that is,
as if disciplinary techniques had begun to be seen as
technical means of conducting the conduct of others and
sometimes, indeed, of oneself (although Foucault pays
relatively little attention to this second aspect, at least at
this stage in his work).[5] Disciplinary techniques were
now regarded, in other words, as generalizable instruments of what, in his later writings, he would call 'government'. Discipline

> was never more important or more valorised than at
> the moment when it became important to manage a
> population; the managing of a population not only
> concerns the collective mass of phenomena, the level
> of its aggregate effects, it also implies the manage-
> ment of a population in its depths and its details.
> (Foucault 1991, p. 102)

The idea that the conduct of others (and of oneself) can
be subjected to instrumental control is clearly predicated
on an orientation which Heidegger describes as 'the essence of technology'. This orientation treats the world as

consisting essentially of forces that can be harnessed, at least in principle, to human purposes. Human individuals and human aggregates, too, will thus be seen, like all other phenomena, as if they were a standing reserve of energy to be put to use.[6] But before this can happen, what it is that will be used in this way – what Heidegger refers to as 'a calculable coherence of forces' (Heidegger 1978, p. 303) – must first be defined and identified. For this reason, Foucault insists that the expansion of discipline in this period goes hand-in-hand with the invention of the humanist subject; that is, of the conception of the human individual as endowed with a soul, consciousness, guilt, remorse, and other features of an interiority that can be worked on by other agents. This humanist subject came to be seen as the locus of usable energy and, therefore, as the focus of instrumental control: the focus, in other words, of discipline.

As Foucault presents it, the attempt to employ discipline in some specific context must suppose that the relevant forces – the human entities over which that discipline will be exercised – have been correctly identified. Discipline, in other words, is always predicated on a claim to knowledge concerning the character of the human subject. Given this claim, the effect of disciplinary failure is to suggest, not that the exercise of discipline itself is mistaken, but rather that there is a need for more knowledge about the person or persons to be acted on. This, in turn, leads to a further refinement of technique. It is in this sense that Foucault regards the idea of prison reform, for example, as 'virtually contemporary with the prison itself: it constitutes, as it were, its programme' (Foucault 1979a, p. 234). In the context of a technological orientation, projects of disciplinary refinement and reform are part and parcel of the understanding of discipline. In addition, since the use of discipline is predicated on a claim to knowledge, disciplinary refinement and reform will often involve corresponding changes in the relevant fields of knowledge. More generally, the disciplinary presumption that individuals and collectivities can usefully be regarded as calculable and manipulable sets of forces suggests both a sense in which the spread of disciplinary techniques, their successes and their failures, promotes the development of knowledge and a sense in which the development of certain kinds of knowledge can promote the spread of discipline. In this respect, Foucault suggests, there is an intimate relationship between the development of disciplinary power on the one hand and the development of certain fields of knowledge on the other. Notable examples of the latter, of course, are what came to be known as the social and behavioural sciences.[7]

Foucault suggests that the perception of discipline as a generalizable instrument of government appears at its most ambitious in the eighteenth-century 'military dream of society':

> its fundamental reference was not to the state of nature, but to the meticulously subordinated cogs of a machine, not to the primal social contract, but to permanent coercions, not to fundamental rights, but to indefinitely progressive forms of training, not to the general will but to automatic docility. (Foucault 1979a, p. 169)

He does not claim that this dream has ever actually been realized in a society subject to meticulous and effective disciplinary control. Rather, he suggests that the dream itself can be seen as elaborating on the idea of discipline as a solution to the general problem of government.

Since it involves the treatment of individuals as a standing reserve of energy, this disciplinary perspective on government contrasts strongly with the representation of governmental power as a function of consent (considered in chapters 2 and 3 above). Nevertheless, it might be tempting to regard the use of discipline, at least in Western societies, not so much as involving a distinct rationality of government, but rather as supplementing a more fundamental mode of governmental power: one that is, in fact, based on right and obligation. In this case, the governmental significance of discipline would be understood as consisting primarily of its use within limited and clearly circumscribed contexts; for example, in the workings of the military and other specialized government agencies, and in the organization of schools, prisons and other institutions for those unable to exercise the rights of citizens. On Foucault's account, however, this perception of the place of discipline in Western societies would be seriously misleading. Discipline certainly is employed in such specialized contexts, but its use is not restricted to them. On the contrary, Foucault presents discipline and its associated techniques of surveillance, regimentation and classification as ubiquitous features of all modern societies. They are ubiquitous, in his view, precisely because discipline itself is regarded in these societies as a generalizable technology of government, one whose use is not confined to any particular techniques or institutional settings. Details of the life of each inhabitant are recorded in the files of numerous public and private agencies, much of their behaviour is subject to routine observation and regulation, and information obtained in this way is commonly used in attempts to influence their conduct.

It is not Foucault's intention to suggest that the imposition of discipline will always achieve the desired effects. On the contrary, he argues that discipline will often be unsuccessful in its aims, and that it will often be resisted. Nevertheless, Foucault offers an account of contemporary Western societies in which each of us is depicted as having learned to take our surveillance, regimentation and classification as a matter of course, and in which our personalities and behaviour are seen as having been moulded accordingly. The suggestion is, then, that we live in a world of disciplinary projects, many of which cut across other such projects, and all of which suffer from more or less successful attempts at resistance and evasion. The result is a disciplinary, but hardly a disciplined, society. In Foucault's view, the pervasive effects of living in such a society go far beyond the purposes for which discipline may be employed in any particular case.

Pastoral Power

Foucault uses the terms 'pastoral power' and 'the shepherd–flock game' to refer to what he sees as an influential view of government: one which understands government in terms of the metaphor of the shepherd and his flock. The metaphor implies that the aim of government is to promote the well-being of its subjects by means of detailed and comprehensive regulation of their behaviour. The shepherd exercises pastoral power over his flock, implying a relationship between ruler and ruled which is more intimate, and more continuous, than any of the standard models of government by consent would allow. Pastoral power, as Foucault presents it, is concerned more with the welfare of its subjects than with their liberty. He claims, for example, that the shepherd–flock metaphor is entirely alien to the clear concern for liberty that we find in both the contractarian and the republican traditions of Western political thought, and that it plays little part in classical Greek and Roman political thought.[8] Many contemporary Western readers will be familiar with the theme from their knowledge of the Old

Testament history of the Jewish people and later Christian elaborations of that history.

Foucault suggests that the Old Testament metaphor of the shepherd and his flock implies a view of relations between ruler and ruled which involves considerably more than the laws and associated sanctions found in the view of sovereign power as based on consent. Three points are central to the contrast which he draws between these two views. First, the shepherd governs a flock and each of its members, rather than a territory and each of its inhabitants. Secondly, the flock exists in and through the activity of its shepherd: remove the shepherd, and the flock is likely to collapse into a mass of dispersed individuals. In contrast, he suggests, the idea of government as working primarily through law and sanction assumes that the community has a life of its own, comprising a multiplicity of activities and relationships that are independent of government.[9] Thirdly, the shepherd cares for the flock both individually and collectively, attending to the needs of its members. This means that the shepherd treats members of his flock according to the particular circumstances of the individual concerned. In contrast, the image of rule on the basis of consent offers a relatively undifferentiated account of the relationship between a government and its citizen-subjects. Underlying the contrast between the two views is the perception of the shepherd (in the pastoral model) as a superior type of being, who may therefore require the sheep to act without the need for consent on their part. In this respect, pastoral power contrasts markedly with the view of sovereign power as based on consent.

Perhaps the clearest example of this 'pastoral' rationality of government is to be found in the theory of police and the associated science of cameralism, both of which were developed most systematically in continental

Europe during the seventeenth and eighteenth centuries.[10] Most readers of this book, especially those brought up in the common law administrations of Britain, North America and Australasia, are likely to think of the police as an organization whose role is essentially constabulary: keeping the peace, protecting innocent persons from harm, and arresting wrongdoers. While some may doubt that police forces always keep to that role, and while others may question the effectiveness with which they pursue it, neither of these equivocations undermines the fact that police are conventionally identified with these constabulary functions.

However, the word 'police' once had a much broader usage. It referred both to an area of government administration – covering everything apart from justice, finance, the army and diplomacy – and to the objectives of that administration. In effect, police was responsible for the comprehensive regulation of social life in the interests of the development of society and the improvement of individuals, and it was expected to pursue these objectives in the most rational fashion. In accordance with this usage, Blackstone's *Commentaries on the Laws of England* of 1783 refers to 'public police and oeconomy' as meaning

> the due regulation and domestic order of the kingdom: whereby the individuals of the state, like members of a well-governed family, are bound to conform their general behaviour to the rules of propriety, good neighbourhood, and good manners; and to be decent, industrious, and inoffensive in their respective stations. (Blackstone, 1978, p. 162)

'Police', in this sense of the term, was not necessarily regarded as the responsibility of the state alone.[11] Indeed, in Britain towards the end of the eighteenth century, the notion of police had come to include 'all those items of the national welfare not completely or adequately handled by public officials' (Andrews 1989, p. 6). The work of philanthropy was particularly significant in this respect: it was intended not only to care for the less fortunate by easing their condition and guiding them in the paths of righteousness, but also to benefit society as a whole. Or, as Andrews puts it:

> a good national 'police' was not to be achieved solely by politicians or by a professional corp of 'police', but by publicly concerned, philanthropically minded citizens. (ibid., p. 7)

The theory of police exemplifies the comprehensive responsibility for the welfare of the flock and each of its members that is central to Foucault's account of the 'pastoral' rationality of government. But there is a further significant aspect of Foucault's treatment of the pastoral theme that should be noted here. This concerns his suggestion that Christianity modified the earlier Hebrew shepherd–flock metaphor in several important respects. Christian ideas of sin, atonement and salvation, for example, added to the moral complexity of relations between the shepherd and each member of the flock. However, the more important modifications, as far as Foucault's argument is concerned, involve the Christian appropriation of the Stoic practice of self-examination in such a way as to bring it together with the guidance of conscience. In the Hellenistic world, Foucault suggests, the guidance of conscience took the form of taking, and perhaps paying for, advice in difficult and unusual circumstances. Christian pastorship, on the other hand, employed self-examination to turn the guidance of conscience into an integral part of a continuous relationship between the shepherd (or his local representative) and each member of the flock. Where the Stoic practice turned self-awareness in upon itself, Christianity used self-examination to expose the individual to more effective guidance and observation. It organized 'a link between total obedience, knowledge of oneself, and confession to someone else' (Foucault 1981, p. 239).

Foucault's suggestion here is that the model of pastoral power which became influential in the West was first developed in the early church. It was later adopted, along with elements of republicanism,[12] by government in the confessional states of seventeenth-century Europe. In fact, the 'pastoral' use of confession, self-examination and guidance continue to be found today, not only in Christian churches and sects, but also in the work of a variety of specialized state agencies and private charitable and philanthropic organizations, in many kinds of counselling, therapy and techniques of personality modification, and, of course, in the personnel development and training practices of many public and private corporations. In such cases, the training of individuals in the exercise of self-government serves as an instrument of the government of their conduct.

In effect, Foucault maintains that both the policing and the confessional aspects of the pastoral model have continued to play a fundamental role in the development of the characteristically modern form of Western government, and especially in the development of a mode of power that aims to rule individuals in a continuous and permanent fashion. Cameralism and the theory of police had a major impact on the development of public administration in France and Germany, where they remained influential well into the late nineteenth century. Nevertheless, its attempt to comprehend almost every aspect of the internal administration of society laid the theory of police open to criticism on a variety of grounds. Some of these are particularly relevant to Foucault's treatment of liberalism and I will consider them in the following section. For the moment, it is important to recognize that, as with his earlier discussion of discipline, Foucault's treatment of the shepherd–flock game is not intended to suggest that this was ever the only, or even the most important, of the Western rationalities of government. His point, rather, is that this model has been, and still remains, an influential governmental rationality in the societies of the modern West. Foucault's discussion clearly suggests, for example, that the pastoral image of government has played an important part in the development of what would now be called the welfare state.

I have already noted that, in its 'policing' aspect, the pastoral model of government makes no presumption of consent on the part of the sheep. In this respect, such a model contrasts strongly with that of a political power resting on the consent of the people, as set out in Locke's *Second Treatise*. The 'confessional' aspect of the pastoral theme, on the other hand, presents us with a variation on the image of the individual as malleable creature of social conditions set out in Locke's *Essay*. In Foucault's terms, the 'pastoral' use of confession, self-examination and guidance of conduct should be seen as instruments of government that work in part through the formation of individuals who can normally be relied upon to impose an appropriate rule on their own behaviour.

Liberty and the Liberal Rationality of Government

If his treatment of discipline and pastoral power as rationalities of government seem to pose problems for standard accounts of governmental power in terms of notions of consent, right and obligation, what Foucault has to say about liberalism poses similar problems in a more acute form. Liberalism is commonly understood as a political doctrine or ideology concerned with the maximization of individual liberty and, in particular, with the defence of natural liberty against the encroachments of the state. If government is regarded primarily as the work of the state, then liberalism, in this sense, is a doctrine of limited government, one which insists that the form and the activities of the state should be understood primarily in terms of their consequences for individual freedom. On this view, the state has two countervailing aspects: on the one hand, it is thought to be necessary to provide the conditions under which the liberty of individuals can be preserved (the rule of law, some reasonable degree of civil peace, defence against invasion, and so on), while on the other, it is regarded as posing a threat to individual liberty, either through the abuse of its necessary powers or through the acquisition of governmental powers of other kinds. It is in this second respect, for example, that democracy is often said to represent a potential threat to liberty since, in their efforts to win popular support, those who compete for political office may be tempted to promise governmental programs that can be pursued only at the expense of liberty itself.[13] Understood in this sense, liberalism requires that government be limited in the interests of individual liberty. The fundamental problem of liberal government, then, is to build the appropriate restraints into a system of government that nevertheless remains sufficiently powerful to secure the liberty of its subjects.

Foucault's discussions of government in general as the conduct of conduct, and of liberalism as a distinctive rationality of government, provide a very different perspective on the character of liberty as a governmental imperative. Since, in Foucault's view, the exercise of power requires a degree of freedom on the part of its subjects, there is a sense in which governmental power must always work through the behaviour of free persons. What is most distinctive about the liberal rationality of government, as Foucault describes it, is not so much its recognition of this elementary fact but, rather, its belief that the long-term objectives of government are best pursued through the free decisions of individuals. Instead of viewing the freedom of its subjects as a potential threat to the work of government – of a kind, for example, that might be dealt with through an appropriate system of police regulation and control – the liberal rationality requires that the state should act to promote that freedom.

As with his work on government, much of what Foucault has to say on this issue remains unpublished, although there are now a number of useful accounts of his arguments.[14] Perhaps the most important feature of his discussion, at least for the purposes of this chapter, concerns the question of 'security'. Liberalism, as Foucault describes it, regards society as containing a number of 'natural' processes – those to do with the economy, the growth of population and so on – and it aims to *secure* the conditions under which those processes will continue to best effect:

the setting in place of . . . . mechanisms or modes of state intervention whose function is to assure the security of those natural phenomena, economic processes and the intrinsic processes of population: this is what becomes the basic objective of governmental rationality. Hence liberty is registered not only as the right of individuals legitimately to oppose the power, the abuses and usurpations of the sovereign, but also now as an indispensable element of governmental rationality itself. (Foucault on 5 April 1978, quoted in Gordon 1991, pp. 19–20)

In order to show how such governmental concern for security can result in a commitment to individual liberty, let me begin by exploring the liberal critique of police. If liberalism is understood as a political doctrine or ideology on the lines set out in the opening paragraph of this section, then the general character of that critique should be clear: the comprehensiveness of police attempts at regulation – the fact that they are aimed at the entire population – must be rejected on the grounds that the primary objective of the state should be the defence of individual liberty, not the pursuit of happiness. This liberal argument against detailed and comprehensive regulation of behaviour is not an argument against regulation as such. Rather, it clears the ground for regulation of the kind set out, for example, in Locke's proposals for reform of the Poor Law administration (considered in chapter 4), in which the ideal of a suitably independent individual provides a norm against which it is possible to measure the conditions and the behaviour of particular individuals, communities and groups. In effect, then, this liberal critique proposes to displace the comprehensive regime of police regulation with a variety of specialized regimes, aiming either to control those minorities whose behaviour is seen to contravene significant social norms, or to secure those norms themselves (for example, through programs of mass education). I shall return to this issue below.

However, Foucault's primary concern is with a different kind of liberal critique of police: one which seeks to address severely practical questions of government. We can see what is at issue here by considering the critique of police set out by Adam Smith early in the discussion of police in his *Lectures on Jurisprudence* (1762–3). Smith observes that 'those cities where the greatest police is exercised are not those which enjoy the greatest security' (Smith 1978, p. 332), and notes that the level of crime and disorder often appears to increase in proportion to the extent of police regulation. However, he claims that it would be wrong to conclude from this that police regulation causes crime; rather, he argues, crime is caused by a lack of freedom within the population.

> Nothing tends to corrupt and enervate and debase the mind as dependency, and nothing gives such noble and generous notions of probity as freedom and independency. (ibid., p. 333)

The best way to minimize crime and disorder, then, is not to increase the number of police but, rather, to promote 'freedom and independency' and, most especially, to reduce the number of servants and retainers. Smith's concern with the problems caused by servants and retainers will have little resonance in Western societies today. Nevertheless, many twentieth-century commentators make similar claims about the demoralizing effects of state welfare provision, contrasting the dependency of welfare recipients to the sturdy independence of those whose living is obtained through the market.

I noted at the beginning of this section that liberalism is commonly regarded as a doctrine which insists on the importance of limited government (in the sense of government by the state) largely as a result of a prior commitment to the maximization of individual liberty. Foucault's analysis of the liberal rationality of government as organized around a concern for security provides a second important sense in which liberalism should be seen as a doctrine of limited government. I have already noted that in his critique of police, Smith treats the market as a source of personal independence. Elsewhere in his *Lectures on Jurisprudence*, and again in *The Wealth of Nations*, Smith argues further that detailed regulation of economic activity in the manner of police will often be counterproductive and detrimental to the goal of national economic improvement. Smith represents the realm of economic activity *first* as a system with a life of its own, operating according to its own laws and functional exigencies, and *secondly*, as constituted in large part by the free choices of a multitude of economic actors. On this view, the freedom of economic actors to choose for themselves is seen to be an essential condition of the functioning of the system as a whole: in the absence of external interference, the prices of goods and services will both determine, and be determined by, these free choices.

The liberal perception of the economy as a system constituted by the free decisions of individuals suggests that the effective workings of government will depend on its ability to secure the conditions under which free persons can pursue their own objectives. Considered as a rationality of government, liberalism maintains not only that the ability of central government to pursue certain kinds of objectives will be limited by the character of the economy (and by the character of such other aspects of social life which may also be understood as self-regulating systems), but also that a central government which respects those limits is likely to be more effective than one which does not. On this liberal view, limited government is a recipe for success while unlimited government is a recipe for failure.

In Foucault's terms, then, the liberal rationality of government regards the liberty of its subjects as an indispensable element of government itself. This view marks a radical departure from the 'pastoral' rationality that characterizes the theory of police. Where police regulation involves making people do what is good for them, even when they may not see it as such, the liberal commitment to liberty requires that they be allowed to choose what is good for themselves. Nevertheless, the

understanding of limited government which this liberal
rationality entails, should not be taken to imply a commitment to the absence of governmental regulation. The
issues here can be dealt with briefly, since I have already
noted most of the essential points in my discussion of
Locke's account of political power.

While Locke insists that all men have an equal right to
their natural liberty – and in that respect he might be
regarded as a liberal before his time – he also maintains
that they are, nevertheless, born 'ignorant and without
the use of *Reason*' (*Second Treatise*, §57; 1988, p. 305).
We have seen that Locke introduces this observation in
the course of his argument that the case for the power
which parents may exercise over their children cannot be
extended to justify the claim to absolute power of a king
over his subjects. However, since this argument implies
that individuals can exercise their natural liberty only if
they have already acquired 'the use of *Reason*', the observation itself has a broader significance. We have also
seen that, in his *Essay*, Locke treats the acquisition of the
use of Reason as if it were primarily a matter of developing the appropriate habits of thought and behaviour
and, especially, of developing the capacity 'to suspend
the prosecution of this or that desire' (*Essay*, Book II, ch.
XXI, §47; 1957, p. 263) while reflecting on a future
course of action. In his educational writings and his
proposals for reform of the Poor Law administration,
Locke addresses what, in Foucault's terms, might be
called the governmental implications of the view that the
requisite habits will not necessarily be acquired simply as
a matter of course.[15] Here, Locke considers the techniques that educators might use to promote in others the
habits of thought and behaviour appropriate to the actions of free persons, the techniques that might be used
by individuals to train themselves in these habits, and the
techniques that might be used by administrators to break

the bad habits of their charges and to promote new ones in their place.

The corresponding problem for what Foucault presents as the liberal rationality of government is that members of the relevant population cannot always be expected to have developed the thought and behaviour habits of 'free' and 'independent' persons: that is, those habits required for the proper functioning of households, markets and other aspects of social life. While, in Foucault's view, liberalism certainly aims to free people from police and other forms of control by the state, it is also concerned to ensure that people's public and private behaviour will be conducted according to appropriate standards of civility, reason and orderliness. Under a liberal regime, therefore, we can expect to find attempts at indirect regulation according to these standards. This indirect regulation operates through such means as the education of individuals so that they are able to analyse and thereby to regulate their own behaviour,[16] and through the design of public buildings and spaces so as to ensure (in the manner of Locke's law of opinion and reputation) that the behaviour of individuals is regulated by the normative gaze of their fellows.[17] At a rather different level, we should also expect to find the development of routines for dealing with deviant cases: those families thought to provide a poor environment for the care and, especially, the socialization of children, immigrants who may not know the language, long-term unemployed people in danger of losing the habits of discipline required for regular employment, unemployed youth who may never have learned those habits, and so on.[18]

I noted earlier that there seems to have been a substantial shift in Foucault's treatment of power, from the power-as-domination approach that appears in *Discipline and Punish* and the first volume of the *History of*

Sexuality to the more complex and nuanced approach found in his work on governmentality and the care of the self. Nevertheless, Foucault's later work on government – and on liberalism, in particular, as a distinctive rationality of government – effectively provides us with a more sophisticated version of the earlier picture. In place of the pervasive effects of discipline, an equally pervasive governmental management of freedom is invoked, to similar effect. On this later view, what makes it possible for the free inhabitants of contemporary Western societies to be governed by the state via mechanisms that appear to rest on their consent is the fact that the vast majority of those inhabitants have already been trained in the dispositions and values of responsible autonomy. The difference between this perspective on the relationship between freedom and government, and that found in the 'radical' view of Lukes and critical theory will be taken up in my concluding chapter.

Government and Political Power

I began this chapter by referring to Foucault's assertion that political theory needs 'to cut off the King's head' (Foucault 1980, p. 121). This assertion is directed at a number of targets, but one of the most significant is the conception considered at length in the earlier chapters of this book: the conception of government as the work of a sovereign power that is founded on, and operates through, the consent of its subjects. Foucault, on the other hand, suggests, first, that the work of government is performed by both state and non-state agencies, and secondly, that government is far more intimately involved in moulding the public and private behaviour – and even the personalities – of individuals than any conception of those individuals as citizens would allow.

We have seen, for example, that Foucault's elaboration of the shepherd–flock metaphor offers a view of the relationship between ruler and ruled that is considerably more complex than that implied by any model of government as operating on the basis of consent. Where the latter model regards citizens (but not necessarily other subjects) as autonomous moral agents, the former treats the personalities of its subjects as open both to detailed regulation and to formation and reformation by governmental action. Where the latter presents a relatively undifferentiated account of the relationship between government and citizen-subjects, and of the political powers through which that relationship will be conducted, the former suggests that both the relationship and the relevant powers will be differentiated according to the particular circumstances of the subject in question. Government, according to the shepherd–flock model, assigns its subjects to appropriate identities and treats them accordingly (as prosperous or poor, healthy or unhealthy, employed or unemployed, one of a couple or a single parent, well-behaved or criminal, sane or mentally ill); or rather, it treats them as more precisely differentiated cases within these general categories. In a liberal adaptation of the shepherd–flock model, the idea (derived from the city–citizen game) of the rational individual provides a norm against which the situation of many of the deviant others can be measured.

It might be tempting – as I noted above with respect to discipline – to regard the pastoral activities of government in contemporary Western societies as if they merely supplemented the operations of a sovereign power that is based primarily on right and obligation. For example, the fact that agencies of the state in these societies have assumed considerable responsibility for the provision of welfare is often understood in terms of a broadly republican view of relations between *the* government and its citizens. A well known elaboration of this view is found in Marshall's (1950) depiction of modern British social policy as operating to secure the rights involved in what he sees as the full realization of citizenship.[19] On the one hand, according to Marshall, the social right to an extended period of childhood education ensures that all adult members of the community are provided with the knowledge and skills expected of citizens. On the other hand, through policies on housing, welfare and income support, the system of social rights ensures that citizens are not prevented by poverty or misfortune from participating in the life of the community. In Marshall's account, then, the fundamental purpose of social policy is to complement the legal and political rights of citizens by securing the conditions under which all adult members of the community are able to participate as independent persons in its affairs.

According to Foucault's analysis of government as structured, at least in part, by the shepherd–flock model, this Marshallian view of social policy seems altogether too anodyne. Thus, Foucault describes the 'welfare state problem' as 'one of the extremely numerous reappearances of the tricky adjustment between political power wielded over legal subjects and pastoral power wielded over live individuals' (Foucault 1981, p. 235). There is more to the pastoral work of government, as Foucault understands it, than the mere provision by the state of knowledge, skills and services to citizens. This is, first, because much of the work of government is performed by non-state agencies, and secondly, because that work also includes individualizing regimes of discipline and supervision, and the use of techniques aimed at the formation of personalities and households with what are thought to be desirable attributes and characteristics.[20] On Foucault's account, then, the use of disciplinary and pastoral techniques goes far beyond the specific contexts of custodial and welfare institutions, and their effects are now pervasive aspects of life in almost all contemporary societies.

This view of the significance of pastoral power in the societies of the modern West suggests that the various models of government as based on, and operating through, the consent of its citizen-subjects provide incomplete – and even seriously misleading – accounts of the governmental powers employed by the state. This sense of the incompleteness of such orthodox accounts is reinforced by Foucault's treatment of liberalism as a rationality of government concerned with the practical problems of managing the behaviour of free persons and securing the basic conditions of their freedom by means of a variety of governmental practices. A liberal government may pursue these objectives by promoting, for example, the existence of properly functioning markets, the provision of training in appropriately tailored techniques of self-understanding and self-mastery, and the provision of sources of expert advice on complex issues of personal conduct. The character of the population as consisting largely of free persons of the appropriate kind thus appears not only as a fundamental presupposition of liberal governance, but also as one of its most important practical accomplishments.

Finally, any model of government as a function of consent is undermined by Foucault's insistence on treating questions concerning the state and its activities in the context of specific rationalities of government. This suggests, in particular, that the state and state instrumentalities should not be regarded as the only agencies of government. Far from being restricted to actions of *the* government, in Foucault's view the government of societies takes place in a variety of state and non-state contexts. The family, for example, can be seen not only as a potential object of government policy, but also as a means of governing the behaviour of its own members. Similarly, accountancy and psychiatry can be seen as regulating behaviour in ways that interact with, but are nevertheless distinct from, regulation through the making and enforcing of laws.

The conceptualization of government in these kinds of terms has devastating consequences for the understanding of power set out in previous chapters and adopted, with the notable exception of the positions considered in chapter 4, by the greater part of contemporary social and political theory. The most significant aspect of that understanding for the present discussion is its presumption that what Locke calls a right of making Laws and a right of defending the commonwealth from injury, are the most important powers of government, in terms of both their practical effectiveness and their normative significance. The Foucauldian account both of the variety of governmental activities and of their dispersion far beyond what might be seen as the institutions of the state brings this presumption into question, and simultaneously casts doubt on the understandings of government and politics which it sustains.[21]

In fact, Foucault's claim that the work of government cannot be reduced to the making and enforcing of laws and to defence is found much earlier in the Weberian analysis of bureaucracy. Weber undermined the legislature–executive model of government with his argument that the distinctive skills and specialized knowledges of the bureau represent a form of power which can never entirely be subordinated by its supposed political masters. The Foucauldian analysis extends the scope of Weber's argument: first, by insisting that significant aspects of the work of government are conducted outside the state bureaucracy and, secondly, by pointing to forms of power associated with other (non-bureaucratic) forms of expertise such as accountancy, economics and psychiatry.[22] On this view, then, there is far more to government in the modern West than most of us have normally been prepared to acknowledge: there is, in other words, considerable 'political power beyond the state' (Rose and Miller 1992).

6

Conclusion

I began this book by suggesting that two conceptions of power have dominated Western political thought in the modern period. One, which has been especially prominent in recent academic discussion, is the conception of power as a simple, quantitative capacity. The notion of power as capacity is often attributed to Hobbes, who defines the 'power of a man' as 'his present means to obtain some future apparent Good' (*Leviathan*, ch. X; 1968, p. 150). On this definition, power is unremarkable: it is simply the capacity to pursue at least some of one's objectives. The possession of power in this sense is therefore a necessary condition of human agency, and power is a ubiquitous feature of human existence. Once this last point has been made, it seems that there is little more that can usefully be said about power defined in this way. It refers to attributes, capacities and possessions that need have nothing in common other than the fact that they might prove useful in the pursuit of human purposes.

In practice, Hobbes and many subsequent students of power have gone beyond the simplicity of this formal definition. They have interpreted power not simply as a capacity, but as a capacity that can itself be apprehended in *quantitative* terms. Thus, Hobbes often writes as if power, as defined above, could also be understood as a quantitative and cumulative phenomenon somewhat analogous to physical force – thereby suggesting that, in the event of conflict, those with more power will

invariably prevail over those with less. This usage requires a sense of the effectiveness of power – indeed a
sense of determinism – which is not necessarily implied
by Hobbes' own definition. It also suggests a sense of the
homogeneity of power: a sense that, beneath the diversity
of resources that might be employed in pursuit of human
purposes, there lurk quantities of some common substance. Power is here conceived as a generalized capacity
or essence of effectiveness which is bestowed on individuals and collectivities by virtue of the resources which
they happen to possess. On this interpretation, power is
not itself a resource; rather, power is what resources of
diverse kinds have in common. Resources, as Giddens
puts it, 'are the media through which power is exercised'
(Giddens 1979, p. 91).

However, I have been more concerned in this book to
stress the importance in Western political thought of a
second, equally 'Hobbesian', conception of power. Within this conception, the idea of power as a capacity is
brought into an equivocal relationship with that of
power as a right. This results from the understanding
that political or sovereign power rests on the obligation
of its subjects to obey, so that the holder of such power
appears to have both the capacity and the right to call on
their obedience. In the modern period, that obligation
has commonly been seen not (or not primarily) as or-
dained by God, but rather as based more or less directly
on the consent of the subjects in question. This conception of power as resting on consent is the key to the
tradition of normative political theory which Foucault is
determined to reject.

Hobbes' model of sovereign power requires a considerably more radical departure from the simplicity of his
formal definition of power than does his interpretation of
power as quantitative capacity noted above. He introduces sovereign power as if it were a power that com-

bines the separate powers of many individuals; that is, as if it were a power in the sense of the quantitative understanding of his initial definition. But he goes on to describe it as constituted in and through numerous presumed acts of consent, in each of which an individual agrees to transfer the right to govern his or her behaviour to the sovereign. Consent, in other words, is seen as giving the sovereign the right to govern its subjects and also, since they have agreed to follow their sovereign's instructions, as giving the sovereign the capacity to do so. On this view, while there may be some who refuse to follow their sovereign's instructions, they can always be dealt with by means of the overwhelming, combined powers which the obedience of the consenting majority places in the sovereign's hands. Hobbes' concept of sovereign power, then, involves a slippage between the idea of power as a capacity and the idea of power as a right. I identified a related slippage in Locke's account of political power both as a right and as something that may exist illegitimately (that is, in the absence of right), as well as in the work of more recent thinkers.

This conception of power as both right and capacity has two important consequences for our conceptualizations of government. First, as I argued in chapter 2, it sustains an influential view of what government is: *the government consists of those members of a political community who can issue instructions which the rest are obliged to obey*. Governments, in other words, are essentially persons and organizations which enact laws and take whatever action is necessary to enforce those laws, although they may also engage in other activities.

Secondly, the fact that two characteristics (both capacity and right) must be present in order for a power to be seen as a power in this sense means that this conception of power as resting on consent commonly involves implicit or explicit reference to other kinds of powers: those

lacking one or other of these characteristics. Thus, while
Hobbes describes sovereign power as resting on consent,
it is clear that consent alone is hardly sufficient to provide the organization required for many individuals to
act according to a single commanding will. Sovereign
power, as Hobbes describes it, must therefore be supplemented by other powers if it is to be effective. Or
again, we have seen that Locke's treatment of a political
power that operates as of right through the invocation of
obligations, leads him to propose a number of alternative
kinds of power. First, his concepts of tyranny and usurpation refer to a power that operates in much the same
way as (legitimate) political power, but without having
the right to do so. Secondly, Locke presents paternal (or
parental) power as properly taking the place of a power
based on consent in conditions where (because of the
legal or mental incapacity of the persons concerned) the
presumption of consent does not apply. Finally, his discussion of morality in the *Essay Concerning Human
Understanding* suggests that a political power (of the
kind set out in his *Second Treatise*) depends on the
workings of the 'Law of Opinion or Reputation', which
is a dispersed form of social regulation independent of
direct central control. I argued in chapter 4 that the idea
of such a dispersed form of regulation underlies both
Lukes' and critical theory's arguments concerning an
illegitimate and insidious power that affects the very
thoughts and desires of its victims, thereby preventing
them, and the society in which they live, from attaining
the condition in which social life may be properly governed on the basis of their consent.

My intention, in this respect, has been not only to note
the existence of these conceptions of power, but also to
demonstrate how they are located in the context of a
normative framework that arises from the primary conception of power as based on consent. Foucault invites us

to reject this conception and the normative framework to which it gives rise.

Accordingly, after three chapters focusing on the vicissitudes of the conception of political power as a function of consent, I turned in chapter 5 to consider the work of Foucault. I began by noting that his most general conception of power, as a 'structure of actions' (Foucault 1980, p. 220) bearing on the actions of individuals who are free, eschews the simple-minded determinism of the conception of power as quantitative capacity. Instead, power is seen as a matter of the instruments, techniques and procedures employed in the attempt to influence the actions of those who have a choice about how they might behave. The exercise of power always involves costs, and its outcome will often be far from certain. It is a trivial consequence of this conclusion that power should be seen neither as essentially centralized and hierarchical, nor as necessarily based on some combination of coercion and consent, nor as always serving a dominant social interest. Some forms of power will be centralized and others dispersed. Some forms of power may presume on consent, others not. In many respects, this view of power is close to that suggested in Hobbes' initial definition, and it shares with that view the clear implication that forms of power may be remarkably heterogeneous. Unfortunately, however, by interpreting power as an underlying essence of effectiveness, Hobbes (and far too many of his successors) is able to acknowledge the heterogeneity of sources of power without recognizing the significance of that heterogeneity. Foucault, on the other hand, concludes that there is little that can usefully be said about power in general.

I noted in chapter 5 that, at least in his later work, Foucault distinguishes between, on the one hand, power in general and, on the other, domination and government, as distinct modalities of the exercise of power. In

his discussions of the latter, Foucault can, in fact, be seen
as presenting a clear alternative to any conceptualization
of political power as a function of consent. Thus, he
ignores altogether questions to do with the legitimacy of
power and focuses instead on influential ways of conceptualizing the practice of governments; that is, on discourses that address practical questions concerning how
to conduct the conduct of others (and of oneself) and,
especially, how to conduct the conduct of the state and
its population. In this light, the notion of a power that
operates on the basis of consent can be seen simply as one
of a number of rationalities of government that have
been influential in the history of the modern West (discipline, pastoral power and liberalism being some of the
others). Foucault's work does, then, appear to provide a
serious alternative to the more orthodox analysis of
power as set out in chapters 2, 3 and 4.

What remains to be considered is the question of how
far Foucault succeeds in escaping from the presuppositions and problems of this more orthodox tradition. I
address this question, first, by considering what might
seem to be a tempting orthodox response to the Foucauldian analysis of government, and, secondly, by exploring
the similarities and differences between Foucault's position and that of critical theory. Finally, I turn to some of
the limitations of Foucault's analysis.

Foucault as Radical Alternative

We have seen that Foucault presents government in
general as the conduct of conduct and, in the particular
case of the state, as the conduct of the conduct of both
the state itself and the population over which the state
claims to rule. While he acknowledges that the enactment
and enforcement of laws are significant aspects of gov-

ernment, Foucault maintains that these activities should not be regarded as the core or essence of government, and therefore as pre-eminent among the ways in which state and non-state agencies attempt to govern the populations of contemporary Western societies. In addition, since the slippery conception of power as both capacity and right has no place in his understanding of government, Foucault avoids altogether those questions of the legitimacy or otherwise of political power that have preoccupied so much of modern political theory.

This kind of position invites an obvious riposte. Even acknowledging that there may be some merit in Foucault's broader understanding of government, could it not be argued that a particular significance should nevertheless be attached to the traditional concern with the legitimacy or otherwise of the institutions and activities of *the* government? I referred in chapter 4 to Wrong's insistence on the importance of distinguishing between 'the exercise of power and social control in general – otherwise there would be no point in employing power as a separate concept or in identifying power relations as a distinct kind of social relation' (Wrong 1979, p. 3). Yet such a distinction is nowhere to be found in Foucault's work (we have already seen that it is also denied by critical theorists). The question to be considered here, then, is whether Foucault's conception of government is so inclusive that there is no point in employing the term to designate a distinct concept or even to identify *the* government as a distinctive institutional structure.

While it may be agreed, for example, that the conduct of conduct is a pervasive feature of contemporary Western societies, it might also be argued that we should distinguish between the exercise of a 'right of making laws' (and of the other powers that Locke associates with that right) and government in Foucault's extended sense of the term. This is, first, because of the particular normative significance that we attach to *government* in the restricted sense and, secondly, because of the overwhelming capacities of the state in contrast to the capacities of other agencies that might also be regarded, in Foucault's understanding of the term, as engaged in the work of government. In addition, while it may well be true that the exercise of government by means of laws and their enforcement requires that the subject population be rendered governable by other means, this claim is also unexceptionable. It is clearly implied, for example, in Locke's discussion of the law of opinion and reputation, and it would not be disputed by a single political theorist of any importance. These points suggest that what Foucault has to offer political theory is something less than the serious challenge set out in the closing section of chapter 5. Rather, his contribution would seem to consist of some useful ideas on how the members of contemporary Western populations have been rendered governable, and a series of interesting questions concerning the intersections of the political and juridical agencies of government on the one hand and a variety of broader 'governmental' practices on the other.

In response to such an objection, it should be noted that Foucault's extended conception of government is considerably less inclusive than Wrong's conception of 'social control in general'. First, government, even in Foucault's most general sense, involves a significant element of calculation that is by no means always present in attempts to influence the behaviour of others. Secondly, Foucault insists that there is a special sense of government which refers to the governing of a state and of the population which that state claims to rule. While government in this special sense is not restricted to the activities of the state itself, we have seen that it nevertheless has a distinctly programmatic character. Thus, when he uses the term to refer to the government of a state, Foucault focuses on the rationalities of government, rather than on the question of its legitimacy. The objection that his usage renders the term so inclusive that it no longer has any distinct meaning is, therefore, misplaced. Rather, Foucault departs from the orthodox usage of the term in his refusal to place the notion of a power that is based on consent at the centre of his analysis of government.

In effect, then, the objection to Foucault's position outlined here amounts to little more than a reassertion of the claim that political power is, or should be, based on the consent of its subjects. Once political power is viewed in such terms then two things follow, as I noted in chapter 2. First, a particular normative significance is seen to attach to the understanding of government as the work of those who make and enforce binding decisions; that is, of *the* government. Secondly, the powers of *the* government are held to be more important than those of other agencies in society. This contrasts starkly with the Foucauldian view that the idea of a sovereign power based on the consent of its subjects should be regarded simply as one rationality of government amongst others that are at play in contemporary societies – and as one that need be accorded no special analytical or explanatory privilege. On this view, while agencies of the state play a major role in the government of these societies, it is misleading to characterize them as operating primarily through mechanisms based on consent.

As we saw in chapter 4, a rejection of the idea that government rests on the consent of its subjects is also central to critical theory's analysis of modern society. Both Foucault and critical theory present Western systems of government by consent as dependent on the population being rendered suitably docile by other means. In fact, several other features suggest that there may be a certain affinity between Foucault's standpoint and that of critical theory. First, Foucault's counterposition of the idea of liberation to that of political *rationality* raises an obvious question concerning the relationship between his discussion and critical theory's analysis of instrumental reason. In particular, aspects of Foucault's treatment of discipline are reminiscent of the concern with the subordination of human individuals to instrumental calculation and control that one finds in the work of Weber and the Frankfurt School. Secondly, while Foucault insists on the creativity of power, a related idea is clearly present in Marcuse's treatment of the imposition of false needs. Such needs have, in his view, turned liberty itself 'into a powerful instrument of domination' (Marcuse 1972, p. 21). Finally, where Foucault insists on the ubiquity of power relations, the idea that power is present in everyday social interaction is an important part of critical theory's account of that insidious power that operates over people's thoughts and desires through the action of 'collective forces and social arrangements' (Lukes 1974, p. 22).

It is important to clarify here the relationship between these two critical standpoints. The argument of chapter 4 suggests that, while there is a sense in which critical theory presents a radical alternative to the standard accounts of contemporary Western governments as based on consent, it can also be regarded as a sophisticated elaboration within the conventional normative framework: that framework which arises from the view of power as based on consent. For this reason, the obvious parallels between these two standpoints might seem to suggest that Foucault's analysis of power, like that of critical theory, is less radical than it sometimes appears.

In fact, such a conclusion would be misleading. In spite of the obvious parallels noted above, there are also fundamental differences between the accounts of power provided by critical theory and Foucault. The most important of these concern their treatments of two closely related issues: one concerning processes of rationalization in Western societies during the modern period, and the other concerning the ideal of the person as an autonomous moral agent.

Like Weber, critical theory presents an image of instrumental rationality as a worldview that has spread like a plague throughout the major institutional areas of modern Western societies, killing off substantive ethical rationalities and other worldviews in the process. Following on from this, the various discourses that each represent some part of the world as a field of instrumental action are described as just so many symptoms of the one underlying infection, that is, of the worldview or orientation of 'instrumental rationality in general'. I noted in chapter 4 that Habermas modifies this bleak picture by means of a distinction between communicative and instrumental reason in which the former is presented as the more fundamental. This enables him to argue that many of the apparently more destructive consequences of rationalization should really be seen as products of the *distortions* of reason, brought about by capitalism and by the impact of power. It is these distortions of reason that have resulted in the dismal predominance of reason's instrumental modality. By locating these consequences in the conditions under which rationality has developed, rather than in the character of reason itself, Habermas claims to have secured the enlightenment faith in the emancipatory potential of reason against the despair that so clearly affected the later work of the first generation of critical theorists.

Foucault's genealogical histories of madness, medicine and punishment, and his sketch of a genealogy of government, modify the story of rationalization in a very different way. In place of an all-embracing phenomenon of rationalization, Foucault focuses on the emergence of particular *rationalities*. In these terms, the problem is not to establish whether or not people conform to general principles of rationality, but rather 'to discover what kind of rationality they are using' (Foucault 1981, p. 226). Thus, while several processes of 'rationalization' are clearly identified in Foucault's work, he suggests that the connections between these different 'rationalities' should be left open to investigation, without assuming any necessary overall coherence.[1] Rather than approaching such processes of rationalization in terms of their alleged universality, Foucault emphasizes their local and contingent aspects.

There is a real difference between these two perspectives, but its significance should not be exaggerated. In his commentary on Kant's 'What is Enlightenment?' Foucault describes this change of focus from the universal to the singular as a matter of turning the critical Kantian question 'back into a positive one: in what was once given to us as *universal, necessary, obligatory*, what place is occupied by whatever is *singular, contingent, and the product of arbitrary constraints?*' (Foucault 1986a, p. 45; emphasis added). There is a sense of continuity in this comment as well as an insistence on difference. Each term in the first series has its correlate in the second: whatever expresses the universal can also be seen to display its singular aspect, and so on. What is at issue here, then, is not much more than the difference between positive and negative prints taken from the same set of photographs.

However, there does seem to be a far more important difference between critical theory and Foucault concerning the ideal of the person as an autonomous moral agent. Critical theory represents itself as both a continuation and an immanent critique of the political project of the Enlightenment. This means that for critical theory the ideal of the person as an autonomous moral agent, and the correlative ideal of the kind of society required to foster the development of such persons, provide a measure of the impact of a certain kind of illegitimate power (Lukes' third dimension of power) and also define a corresponding project of human emancipation. In effect, the impact of power is identified here in terms of a difference between the real and the postulated ideal. Power, understood in this sense, serves a clear explanatory purpose in critical theory. But this purpose is not to provide an answer to the question 'What happens?'[2] in terms of the effects of identifiable conditions and processes. Rather, power is introduced to explain why the conditions required by the utopian ideal do not exist.

While Habermas and the earlier generation of critical theorists differ over the emancipatory potential of rationalization, they nevertheless share the same emancipatory ideal. In contrast, Foucault proposes no normative ideal of the human person to correspond to critical theory's model of the rational, autonomous moral agent. Indeed, Foucault's account of the individualizing effects of political rationality strongly suggest that any such ideal should be seen, not as evidencing the absence of domination, but rather as one of domination's most fundamental effects.[3] Critical theory's correlative ideal of a society which consists of autonomous individuals and is governed solely on the basis of their rational consent, makes little sense in Foucault's terms. Thus, in a passage which is clearly directed at Habermas's notion of undistorted communication Foucault comments:

> The thought that there could be a state of communication which would be such that the games of truth could circulate freely, without obstacles, without constraint and without coercive effects, seems to me to be Utopia. (Foucault 1988a, p. 18)

In so far as power would play any part in such an Utopia, it would work through rational consent and perhaps

through something like Locke's law of opinion and reputation. This would be a society in which no other significant powers were employed, and in which the personalities of the inhabitants were formed independently of
the exercise of power.

If, as Foucault maintains, power consists in the attempt
to act on the actions of others, then power is an inescapable feature of human interaction. Foucault goes further
to insist that power is often creative, and that some of its
effects appear in the personalities of those who are subject to its exercise. This should not be seen as a matter of
the imposition of false needs, as Marcuse would have it.
On the contrary, because Foucault proposes no normative ideal that corresponds to critical theory's model of
the rational, autonomous individual, he offers no
grounds on which needs (or other personality attributes)
could be said to be either true or false. In effect, Foucault
insists both that power is ubiquitous and that there can
be no personalities that are formed independently of its
effects. His discussions of discipline, and especially of the
techniques of pastoral power, suggest a variety of ways
in which the exercise of power can mould the personalities of individuals.

However, it should be noted that Foucault does not
claim that human subjects are nothing but the products
of power since, as we have seen, he insists that the
exercise of power always presupposes some degree of
freedom on the part of its subjects. This freedom means
first that, just as power itself is an inescapable feature of
human interaction, so too are resistance and evasion. If
resistance to power is inescapable, then it hardly requires
justification. There is therefore little point in the all-too-
common complaint that, in his treatment of power and
resistance, Foucault 'refuses to link the latter to the capacity of competent subjects to say, with reason, "yes" or
"no" to claims made upon them by others' (McCarthy

1992, p. 134). In fact, much of the insistence on resistance in Foucault's work reflects the Nietzschean character of his conception of power. Nietzsche's will to power is also the will to resist constraints imposed by other powers. It is the common condition of all living things: as much an attribute of the mushroom which forces its way up through a layer of concrete as of those human individuals who aim to subordinate others or who choose to risk death in their fight for freedom. To the extent that Foucault celebrates resistance, then, it is a Nietzschean celebration of life itself rather than the expression of any commitment to some emancipatory ideal.[4]

Secondly, the fact that those who are subject to power possess some degree of freedom means also that there is no contradiction between, on the one hand, Foucault's insistence on the ubiquity of power and, on the other, his later emphasis on ethics and on what the third volume of his *History of Sexuality* calls 'the care of the self'. Such an emphasis need not suppose that care of the self requires a generalized emancipation from the continuing effects of power. On the contrary, precisely because subjects always have some degree of freedom, the effects of power will invariably leave room for practices of self-cultivation.

In summary, then, while there are superficial parallels between the work of Foucault on power and government and that of critical theory, there are also a number of crucial differences. The most fundamental of these involves the credence that each gives to the conventional view of power as resting on consent: in Foucault's model such a view quite simply has no place, while in that of critical theory it underpins the emancipatory ideal of a society in which individuals are free from the negative effects of power. This suggests that Foucault can, with some justification, be seen as providing a radical alternative to conventional understandings of power. However, the radical character of his conception is seriously limited in two respects. It is to these that I shall now turn.

Enduring Fictions

As we have seen, Foucault's account of power and its effects appears to undermine any conception of a generalized human emancipation of the kind proposed by critical theory.[5] If power is unavoidable, then there is no point in postulating an imaginary state of emancipation from its effects as a viable normative ideal. However, emancipation from particular systems of power, or from the effects of the employment of particular techniques of power, is another matter entirely. Limited, and specific, emancipations might well be regarded as desirable in some cases. Indeed, after insisting that 'the historical ontology of ourselves must turn away from all projects that claim to be global or radical' (Foucault 1986a, p. 46) Foucault goes on to say:

> I prefer the very specific transformations that have proved to be possible in the last twenty years in a certain number of areas that concern our ways of being and thinking, relations to authority, relations between the sexes, the way in which we perceive insanity or illness . . . (ibid., pp. 46–7)

On Foucault's analysis, the most that can be expected from such particularized reforms is the substitution of one set of powers for another, rather than some apparently universalistic process of emancipation from the effects of power as such.

Unfortunately, things are not so simple. In spite of Foucault's explicit avoidance of any universalistic discourse of emancipation from the effects of power, there are passages in which his treatment of states of domination – that is, 'what we ordinarily call power' (Foucault 1988a, p. 19) – in relation both to liberty and to the critical function of philosophy, seems to resurrect many of critical theory's traditional concerns. I noted in chapter 5, for example, his identification of the critical function of philosophy with 'precisely the challenging of all phenomena of domination' and his claim that this function emerges from the imperative to 'Be concerned with yourself, ie, ground yourself in liberty . . .' (ibid., p. 20).[6] Furthermore, in the same interview, he notes that

> relations of power are not something bad in themselves, from which one must free one's self . . . The problem is not of trying to dissolve them in the utopia of a perfectly transparent communication, but to give one's self the rules of law, the techniques of management, and also the ethics, the *ethos, the practice of self which would allow these games of power to be played with a minimum of domination.* (ibid., p. 18; emphasis added)

Foucault does not object to relations of power in which things could easily be reversed, or to hierarchical practices of pedagogy based upon possession of superior knowledge – provided, of course, that the pupils are not subjected, in addition, to 'the arbitrary and useless authority of a teacher' (ibid.). In another of his interviews he distinguishes between the Greek view of friendship, which he describes as a matter of reciprocity, and their

> ethics of pleasure . . . linked to a virile society, to dissymmetry, exclusion of the other, an obsession with penetration, and a kind of threat of being

dispossessed of your own energy and so on. All that
is quite disgusting! (Foucault 1986b, p. 346)

These, and other such comments, plainly suggest that
Foucault regards domination as, at best, a necessary evil,
and one which is to be avoided as far as possible. It is
clear, also, that his concern is not only with the impact of
domination on the liberty of the dominated, but also
with the condition of those who seek to dominate. The
problem, he insists, is to 'give one's self . . . the techniques of management' that will result in 'a minimum of
domination' (Foucault 1988a, p. 18). Without necessarily endorsing the classical Greek account of care of the
self in its entirety, Foucault clearly sympathizes with the
view that 'if you care for yourself correctly . . . then you
cannot abuse your power over others' (ibid., p. 8).

No doubt Foucault's sentiments in this area are ones
that will widely be shared. Both the counterposition of
liberty to domination in favour of the former, and the
idea that there are costs to oneself in the attempt to
dominate others, are familiar refrains in Western
thought. Where the ideal of liberty is so widely acknowledged, we should not be surprised if domination is seen
as something to be resisted in the name of that ideal.

The difficulty here is that there are passages in which
Foucault seems to suggest not only that domination will
in fact be resisted, but also that it *should* be kept to a
minimum. However, if we take seriously his radical account of the constitution of the subject and of the productivity of power, then it is difficult not to be sceptical
of the way in which he sometimes counterposes liberty to
domination. If, for example, we follow Foucault in regarding human subjects as singular and contingent products who are invariably constituted, at least in part, by
the effects of power – if, in short, heteronomy is indeed
the inescapable condition of human existence – then

there would seem to be no grounds for endorsing, without serious qualification, any condemnation of domination ('what we ordinarily call power', Foucault 1988a, p. 19) in general. In a well-known passage from the second essay of *On the Genealogy of Morals*, Nietzsche argues that:

> The task of breeding an animal with the right to make promises presupposes as a preparatory task that one first *makes* men to a certain degree necessary, uniform, like among like, regular, and consequently calculable. (Nietzsche 1967, Essay 2, §II)

If individuals are to be able to make promises about their future behaviour, they must first be able to treat their own behaviour as something that is calculable and predictable. Nietzsche's point is that this is possible only as the outcome of a long history of discipline and regimentation: it is not a natural human condition that can simply be taken for granted. What matters for the present argument is the implication that Nietzsche's sovereign individual is the 'ripest fruit' of a pervasive system of domination. Domination, in other words, is an indispensable condition of liberty – or at least of the kinds of liberty that we (and Nietzsche) have learned to desire.[7] In fact, we saw in chapter 2 that Hobbes' account of the formation of a Common-wealth arrives at a similar conclusion, albeit from a radically different starting point.[8]

My purpose here is not to endorse the detail of either Nietzsche's or Hobbes' analysis, but rather to highlight a problem in Foucault's treatment of domination. There are powerful arguments to suggest that domination and subjectification are conditions of organized social existence and therefore of such liberty as organized social existence makes possible. It would be difficult to insist, as Foucault certainly does, on the productivity of power in the formation of human attributes and capacities and yet to deny or to condemn the productivity of domination in these same respects. It is one thing to say that domination will, in fact, be resisted, and that in certain contexts it will often be resisted in the name of liberty. It is another thing entirely to suggest that domination of any kind should be kept to a minimum. The first observation carries no normative implications, while the second presents the mere presence of domination as if it were an appropriate object of normative judgement: as something that is bad in itself. The first might be expected to result in proposals for specific transformations and reforms. The second, however, invokes the ideal of a community in which domination is reduced to a minimum. In this respect, it belongs to the class of projects which, as we have seen, Foucault himself condemns for claiming 'to be global or radical' (Foucault 1986a, p. 46). The sweeping condemnation of domination in the name of liberty that Foucault proposes in several of his later interviews and shorter essays serves to promote yet another version of the utopian critique of power that Foucault's own work has done so much to undermine.

Finally, there is a sense in which Foucault's critique of the idea of sovereignty might be regarded as incomplete. As we have seen, Foucault argues that government (in the sense of *the* government) makes use of targeted, individualizing powers as well as of the generalized power of sovereignty, that government of others is a ubiquitous feature of social life, not restricted to *the* government, and that the attributes and personal qualities of subjects should not be regarded as if they were formed independently of the effects of power. To say that governments employ individualizing techniques of power, that power is ubiquitous, and that the qualities of subjects are not independent of its effects is also, of course, to say that the world invoked by the notion of a power based on the rational consent of its subjects is a fiction. Yet it would be misleading to suggest – as Foucault sometimes appears to do – that Western political thought has failed to acknowledge the fictional character of that world. Far from it. The problem is, rather, that while acknowledging it as a fiction, Western political thought nevertheless continues to make use of that world: both as a surrogate for the present, and as a model of what ought to, but does not, exist. The idea of a community of autonomous persons surfaces in the language and institutional framework of democratic government, in the provision of norms for social policy intervention, and in diverse moral critiques of political power. Ironically, as we saw in chapter 4, the fictions invoked by radical critics of current practices are remarkably similar to those invoked by defenders of the same practices.

Chapter 1 of this book referred to Foucault's claim that political theory 'is obsessed with the person of the sovereign' (Foucault 1980, p. 121). In fact, the problem to which it alludes is symptomatic of a more general modern obsession with the idea of the person as autonomous agent, and consequently, with the idea that a community of such persons can, and should, be governed by the consent of its members. Thus, the role attributed to the sovereign in Hobbes' *Leviathan* is itself a consequence of his treatment of the subjects as autonomous persons, ultimately bound by nothing other than their consent to the sovereign's rule. The same can be said of the role of *the* government (that is, the holder of political power) in Locke's *Second Treatise*. In the arguments of critical theory, on the other hand, where the *person* of the sovereign (or of *the* government) plays a more limited role, the ideal of a community of autonomous persons is central to both the understanding and the critique of modern society.

The fictional character of the world invoked by this idea of a community of autonomous persons is not an unrecognized feature of the discourse of political power. Yet, while considerable attention has been paid (by Foucault himself and by many others) to the genealogy of modern conceptions of the human individual, the same can hardly be said of our understandings of the community to which that individual is thought to belong. Serious consideration of this latter issue would take us far beyond the problem of political power to a more general investigation of the role of fictional communities in the social and political thinking of contemporary Western societies. To bring this book to its close, however, it is necessary only to note that Foucault's claim that 'we need . . . a political philosophy that isn't erected around the problem of sovereignty' (Foucault 1980, p. 121) does not go far enough. It is not only the problem of sovereignty that *we* (another fictional community) need to free ourselves from, but also the problem of political community. In effect, this means finding a way to think about politics in the absence of its defining, constitutive fiction: something far easier to suggest than it will be to effect.

Notes

Chapter 1   Introduction

1 Bell et al. 1969 is a useful collection of some of the most important contributions to these debates.
2 See Hinsley, 1986, especially chapter 4.
3 See the concise treatment of the contrast between the subject and the citizen in Balibar 1991.
4 See Habermas 1989 and Keane 1988.
5 Although it has been taken up by a number of English-language academics. See especially, Burchell et al. 1991, and the works of Dean, Miller, Rose and Tully cited in the bibliography.

Chapter 2   'that Mortal God': Hobbes on Power and the Sovereign

1 Since there are many editions of this text my references cite both Hobbes' chapter numbers, which are common to all editions, and the page numbers from Macpherson's 1968 edition. My title comes from ch. XVII; 1968, p. 227.
2 See Wartenberg 1990 for a careful analysis of these and other weaknesses of the quantitative understanding of power.

3 Wartenberg criticizes the dyadic focus of this mechanical model of power on the ground that it abstracts from the fact that power relations 'come into being as the result of the actions of agents who do not themselves figure explicitly in the power dyad itself' (Wartenberg 1992, p. 80).

4 See Lessnoff 1986 for a brief survey of the various forms of contract theory.

5 Nozick 1974 represents the first position, while Rawls 1972 has often been cited in support of the second.

6 See Skinner 1984, 1990, Pocock 1975 and, for discussions of its contemporary relevance, Oldfield 1990, and Braithwaite and Pettit 1992.

Chapter 3 'a Right of making Laws': Locke on Political Power and Morality

1 Since there are many editions of this text my references cite Locke's numbered paragraphs, which are common to all editions, and page numbers from Laslett's 1988 edition. My title comes from §3. References to Locke's *Essay Concerning Human Understanding* follow a similar convention, citing book, chapter and paragraph numbers, and page numbers from Nidditch's 1957 edition.

2 The reference to property here should not be interpreted narrowly. Locke also maintains that 'every Man has Property in his own Person' (§27).

3 See the discussion of this point in Pateman 1988, especially ch. 4.

4 See the discussion in Wartenberg 1990, especially ch. 2.

5 Laslett's edition of the *Two Treatises* (Locke 1988) notes at this point that the American Declaration of Independence has: 'But when a long train of abuses and usurpations pursuing invariably the same object . . .'.

6 We have seen that Hobbes takes a different view; so too, on this point, does Kant. After insisting on the importance

of the idea of the original contract, Kant goes on to say: 'The origin of the supreme power, for all practical purposes, is not discoverable by the people who are subject to it. In other words, the subject ought not to indulge in speculations about its origin with a view to acting upon them, as if its right to be obeyed were open to doubt' (Kant 1970 [1797] p. 143).

7 See the selection in Keane (ed.) 1988 and Keane's own discussion of the issues in Keane 1988.

Chapter 4 'the supreme exercise of power': Lukes and Critical Theory

1 Compare the discussions of Locke's proposals by Beier 1988, Dunn 1989, and Ivison 1993, and Oestreich's 1982 treatment of the revival of Stoicism in this period.

2 Hegel (in *Philosophy of Right*) is often credited with the introduction of a clear distinction between civil society and the state – although Hegel's 'civil society' included governmental institutions (such as police) that would now be regarded as part of the state. The idea of civil society as a sphere of activity distinct from the state was taken up by Marx and many later Marxists and again, in the latter part of the twentieth century, by radicals living under communist regimes – who called for the development of such a civil society – and by radical democrats in the West – who called for the democratization of civil society itself. See Keane 1988 for a brief discussion of these and other views of civil society.

3 I have discussed elsewhere the difficulties involved in the treatment of classes as actors (Hindess 1987a).

4 How far Habermas succeeds in avoiding the difficulties that plagued the earlier generation of critical theorists remains a matter of dispute. See the discussion in Miller 1987.

5 The idea of societal media was first elaborated in Parsons' discussion of power (Parsons 1969a).

Chapter 5   discipline and cherish: Foucault on Power, Domination and Government

1 This account is sometimes regarded as a major statement of his intellectual objectives. In the last interview before he died, Foucault comments that he 'wrote only a very small article on Nietzsche'. Nevertheless he goes on to confess that 'I am simply Nietzschean, and I try to see, on a number of points, and to the extent that it is possible, with the aid of Nietzsche's texts – and also with anti-Nietzschean theses (which are nevertheless Nietzschean!) – what can be done in this or that domain' (Foucault 1988b, pp. 250–1).

2 See the papers by Burchell and Gordon in Burchell et al. 1991 and Dean 1994 (especially ch. 9) for systematic presentations of Foucault's analysis.

3 See the useful survey of the literature on the confessional states of Europe in Hsia 1989.

4 Foucault notes a fourth approach in the first volume of *The History of Sexuality* which refers to 'an explosion of numerous and diverse techniques for achieving the subjugation of bodies and the control of populations, marking the beginning of an era of "bio-power" ' (Foucault 1979b, p. 140).

5 This neglect of self-discipline in Foucault's discussion of the emergence of a widespread concern with the uses of discipline may be a consequence of his failure to distinguish between domination and power at this stage in his work. For a different view of the importance of ideas of self-discipline in this period see Oestreich's (1982) treatment of the revival of stoic ideas in the development of the early modern state.

6 Heidegger comments on the double-edged character of this orientation, noting, in particular, the danger that man 'himself will have to be taken as a standing-reserve. Meanwhile, man, precisely as the one so threatened, exalts himself to the posture of lord of the earth' (Heidegger 1978, p. 308). Closely related concerns with the subordination of

human individuals to instrumental calculation and control underlie much of the ambivalence towards the rationalization of the West that one finds in the work of Weber and the Frankfurt School. Foucault does not refer to Heidegger in *Discipline and Punish*, and there are few references to him elsewhere in Foucault's work. Nevertheless, as with many other 'post-structuralist' writers, the ghost of Heidegger can often be observed lurking in the background. In the interview cited in note 1 above Foucault comments: 'For me Heidegger has always been the essential philosopher . . .' My entire philosophical development was determined by my reading of Heidegger. I nevertheless recognise that Nietzsche outweighed him . . . I think it is important to have a small number of authors with whom one thinks, with whom one works, but about whom one does not write' (Foucault 1988b, p. 250).

7 Since, as I noted earlier, Foucault makes no clear distinction between power and domination at this stage in his work it is important to recognize that this 'power/knowledge' relationship need not imply that the social and behavioural sciences can be seen simply as the servants of domination. Much of the knowledge they provide can be used for disciplinary purposes, but it can also be used in the service of resistance.

8 The pastoral theme is discussed at length in Plato's *The Statesman*, but with the aim of showing that the role of the political leader is *not* to be a shepherd. Cf. Foucault, 1981, pp. 231–5.

9 In fact the contrast is somewhat overdrawn since sheep and goats are herd animals with a rudimentary social structure of their own. The shepherd does not so much create this structure as work through it; for example, by making use of such features as the lead animal.

10 Raeff 1983, Small 1962, Dean 1991, ch. 3. Dean (1991, p. 60) suggests that the limited development of the theory of police in eighteenth-century England may be due to the early growth of a centralized state and to the effective

performance of 'police' functions by local justices of the peace.

11 Hegel's *Philosophy of Right* (published 1821) is generally credited with making the first clear distinction between civil society and the state, but it locates police clearly within the realm of civil society.

12 'Our societies proved to be really demonic since they happened to combine those two games – the city–citizen game and the shepherd-flock game – in what we call the modern states' (Foucault 1981, p. 239). The 'city–citizen game' refers to the republican image of the citizens as being both ruler and ruled.

13 Hayek 1982, especially vol. 3.

14 See papers by Burchell and Gordon in Burchell, et al. 1991 and Burchell 1993. Foucault's analysis of liberalism as a rationality of government has been developed in Dean 1991, the contributions to Burchell et al. 1991 and the special issue on 'Liberalism and Governmentality' of *Economy and Society* (22, 3), and Rose and Miller 1992.

15 See Beier 1988, Dunn 1989, Ivison 1993 and Tully 1989.

16 Hunter 1988, 1994.

17 See Rabinow's 1989 discussion of urban design and Bennett's 1988 analysis of department stores and museums.

18 In these respects it is important to recognize that what Foucault describes as the distinctively *liberal* rationality of government is far from being the atomistic conception of society that Sandel 1982 and other 'communitarian' critics of liberalism claim to have identified. On the contrary, the individuals whose liberty Foucault presents as an indispensable element of liberal governmental rationality are themselves regarded not as isolated units, but rather as members of a population that has been rendered orderly and civilized by the operations of markets and other 'spontaneous' social orders on the one hand and by the work of government on the other.

19 See Marshall 1950 and the discussions in Barbalet 1988 and Turner 1986. I argue elsewhere (Hindess 1993) that

the Marshallian theory of citizenship provides a thoroughly misleading account of contemporary Western societies.

20 Donzelot 1979 provides an interesting elaboration of this perspective.

21 Towards the end of 'The Subject and Power' Foucault maintains that power relations in contemporary societies 'have come more and more under state control' (Foucault 1982, p. 224). While this formulation might seem to suggest that these other powers have been subordinated to those of government in the restricted sense, its significance should not be misinterpreted. Since he denies that the state can be identified with a unitary directing purpose, it amounts to the claim that state agencies of one kind or another, and agencies operating under some form of state regulation, have become increasingly involved in power relations. The suggestion, in other words, is that alongside, and indeed as part of, the governmentalization of the state there has also been a tendency to bring state instrumentalities into broader projects of government.

22 See, for example, the contributions to Burchell et al. 1991, Miller and Rose (eds.) 1986 and the special issue of *Economy and Society* on 'Liberalism and Governmentality', and Rose and Miller 1992.

Chapter 6   Conclusion

1 See the discussions of Weber and Foucault in Gordon 1987 and Hindess 1987b.

2 Compare Foucault's comment that we should be concerned with '"How", not in the sense of "How does it manifest itself?" but "By what means is it exercised?" and "What happens when individuals exert (as they say) power over others?"' (Foucault 1982, p. 217).

3 In his Dartmouth Lectures (Foucault 1993), Foucault suggests that the self should be seen as an artefact of technologies of the self that we have inherited from early Christianity.

4 On this point see especially Patton 1994.
5 Critical theorists have, naturally, been particularly critical of this aspect of Foucault's work. The arguments here have been widely rehearsed, most clearly perhaps in Fraser 1989, McCarthy 1992 and Taylor 1986. For an excellent discussion of the issues here see Patton 1989, and Taylor's response (1989).
6 Compare his commentary on Kant's 'What is Enlightenment?' in which critique is described as 'seeking to give new impetus . . . to the undefined work of freedom' (Foucault 1986a, p. 46).
7 Freud developed a version of this argument in his *Civilisation and its Discontents* which was also taken up by critical theory, notably in Marcuse 1955. Foucault's attack on the repressive hypothesis regarding human sexuality (Foucault 1979b) undermines this Freudian version, but it does little damage to Nietzsche's more general version of the argument.
8 See the discussion of Hobbes and Nietzsche in Patton 1993.

References

Andrews, D. T. 1989: *Philanthropy and Police: London charity in the eighteenth century*. Princeton, New Jersey: Princeton University Press.

Aristotle (ed. Stephen Everson) 1988: *The Politics*. Cambridge: Cambridge University Press.

Bachrach, P. and Baratz, M. S. 1969: Two faces of power. In R. Bell, D. V. Edwards and R. H. Wagner (eds.), *Political Power: a reader in theory and research*. New York: Free Press, 94–9.

Balibar, E. 1991: Citizen subject. In E. Cadava, P. Connor and J.-L. Nancy (eds.), *Who Comes after the Subject?* New York: Routledge, 33–7.

Barbalet, J. 1988: *Citizenship*. Milton Keynes: Open University Press.

Beier, A. L. 1988: Utter strangers to industry, morality and religion: John Locke on the poor. *Eighteenth Century Life*, 12 (3), 28–41.

Bell, R., Edwards, D. V. and Wagner, R. H. (eds.) 1969: *Political Power: a reader in theory and research*. New York: Free Press.

Bennett, T. 1988: The exhibitionary complex. *New Formations*, 4, 73–103.

[167]

Blackstone, W. 1978 [1783]: *Commentaries on the Laws of England*. New York and London: Garland Publishing.

Braithwaite, J. and Pettit, P. 1990: *Not Just Deserts*. Oxford: Oxford University Press.

Burchell, G. 1993: Liberal government and techniques of the self. *Economy and Society*, 22 (3), 267–82.

Burchell, G., Gordon, C. and Miller, P. (eds.) 1991: *The Foucault Effect: studies in governmentality*. Hemel Hempstead: Harvester Wheatsheaf.

Dahl, R. A. 1957: The concept of power. *Behavioural Scientist*, 2, 201–5.

Dahl, R. A. 1958: A critique of the ruling elite model. *American Political Science Review*, 52, 463–9.

Dahl, R. A. 1961: *Who Governs? Democracy and Power in an American City*. New Haven and London: Yale University Press.

Dahl, R. A. 1989: *Democracy and its Critics*. New Haven and London: Yale University Press.

Dean, M. 1991: *The Constitution of Poverty: toward a genealogy of liberal governance*. London: Routledge.

Dean, M. 1994: *Critical and Effective Histories: Foucault's methods and historical sociology*. London: Routledge.

Donzelot, J. 1979: *The Policing of Families*. New York: Pantheon.

Dunn, J. 1989: 'Bright enough for All our Purposes': John Locke's conception of a civilised society. *Proceedings of the Royal Society*, 43, 133–53.

Foucault, M. 1977: Nietzsche, genealogy, history. In D. F. Bouchard (ed.), *Language, Counter-memory, Practice: selected essays and interviews by Michel Foucault*. Ithaca, New York: Cornell University Press, 139–64.

Foucault, M. 1979a: *Discipline and Punish*. London: Allen Lane.

Foucault, M. 1979b: *The History of Sexuality*, Vol. 1, *An Introduction*. London: Allen Lane.

Foucault, M. (ed. Colin Gordon) 1980: *Power/Knowledge*. Brighton: Harvester.

Foucault, M. 1981: Omnes et singulatim: towards a criticism of 'Political Reason'. In S. McMurrin (ed.), *The Tanner Lectures on Human Values, II*. Salt Lake City: University of Utah Press, 223–54.

Foucault, M. 1982: The subject and power. In H. L. Drefus and P. Rabinow (eds.), *Michel Foucault: beyond structuralism and hermeneutics*. Brighton: Harvester, 208–26.

Foucault, M. 1986a: What is Enlightenment? In P. Rabinow (ed.), *The Foucault Reader*. Harmondsworth: Penguin, 32–50.

Foucault, M. 1986b: On the genealogy of ethics: an overview of work in progress. In P. Rabinow (ed.), *The Foucault Reader*. Harmondsworth: Penguin, 340–72.

Foucault, M. 1986c: *The History of Sexuality*, Vol. 3, *The Care of the Self*. London: Penguin.

Foucault, M. 1988a: The ethic of care for the self as a practice of freedom. In J. Bernauer and D. Rasmussen (eds.), *The Final Foucault*. Boston, Mass.: MIT Press, 1–20.

Foucault, M. 1988b: The return of morality. In L. Kritzman (ed.), *Michel Foucault: politics, philosophy, culture*. London and New York: Routledge, 242–54.

Foucault, M. 1991: Governmentality. In G. Burchell et al. (eds.), *The Foucault Effect: studies in governmentality*. Hemel Hempstead: Harvester Wheatsheaf, 87–104.

Foucault, M. 1993: About the beginning of the hermeneutics of the self. *Political Theory*, 21 (2), 198–227.

Fraser, N. 1989: Foucault on modern power: empirical insights and normative confusions. In eadem, *Unruly Practices: power, discourse and gender in contemporary social theory*. Cambridge: Polity, 17–34.

Freud, S. 1948: *Civilization and its Discontents*. London, Hogarth Press.

Giddens, A. 1984: *The Constitution of Society*. Oxford: Polity.

Gordon, C. 1987: The soul of the citizen: Max Weber and Michel Foucault on rationality and government. In S. Lash and S. Whimster (eds.), *Max Weber: rationality and modernity*. London: Allen and Unwin, 296–316.

Gordon, C. 1991: Governmental Rationality: an introduction. In G. Burchell et al. (eds.), *The Foucault Effect: studies in governmentality*. Hemel Hempstead: Harvester Wheatsheaf, 1–52.

Habermas, J. 1973: Wahrheitstheorien. In H. Fahrenbach (ed.), *Festschrift für W. Schulz*. Pfullingen: Neske, 211–65.

Habermas, J. 1989: *The Structural Transformation of the Public Sphere*. Oxford: Polity.

Habermas, J. 1984: *The Theory of Communicative Action*, Vol. 1, *Reason and the Rationalization of Society*. Boston, Mass.: Beacon Press.

Habermas, J. 1987: *The Theory of Communicative Action*, Vol. 2, *The Critique of Functionalist Reason*. Boston, Mass.: Beacon Press.

Habermas, J. 1990: *Moral Consciousness and Communicative Action*. Cambridge: Polity.

Hayek, F. A. von 1982: *Law, Legislation and Liberty*. London: Routledge and Kegan Paul.

Heidegger, M. 1978: The question concerning technology. In D. F. Krell (ed.), *Martin Heidegger: basic writings*. London: Routledge and Kegan Paul, 283–318.

Hindess, B. 1987a: *Politics and Class Analysis*. Oxford, Blackwell.

Hindess, B. 1987b: Rationalization and the characterization of modern society. In S. Lash and S. Whimster (eds.), *Max Weber: rationality and modernity*. London: Allen and Unwin, 137–53.

Hindess, B. 1993: Citizenship in the modern West. In B. Turner (ed.), *Citizenship and Social Theory*. London: Sage, 19–35.

Hinsley, F. H. 1986: *Sovereignty*. Cambridge: Cambridge University Press.

Hobbes, T. 1928 [1640]: *Elements of Law: Natural and Politic*. Cambridge: Cambridge University Press.

Hobbes, T. 1968 [1651]: *Leviathan*. London: Penguin.

Hsia, R. P.-C. 1989: *Social Discipline in the Reformation: Central Europe 1550–1750*. London and New York: Routledge.

Hunter, F. 1953: *Community Power Structure*. Chapel Hill: University of North Carolina Press.

Hunter, I. 1988: *Culture and Government: the emergence of literary education*. Basingstoke: Macmillan.

Hunter, I. 1994: *Rethinking the School*. Sydney: Allen and Unwin.

Ivison, D. 1993: Liberal conduct. *History of the Human Sciences*, 6 (3), 25–59.

Kant, I. 1970 [1797]: *The Metaphysics of Morals*. In idem (ed. H. Reiss), *Political Writings*. Cambridge: Cambridge University Press.

Keane, J. 1988: *Democracy and Civil Society*. London: Verso.

Keane, J. (ed.) 1988: *Civil Society and the State*. London: Verso.

Koselleck, R. 1988: *Critique and Crisis: enlightenment and the pathogenesis of modern society*. Oxford: Berg.

Lessnoff, M. H. 1986: *Social Contract*. London: Macmillan.

Locke, J. 1969 [1697]: A report of the board of trade to the lords justices respecting the relief and employment of the poor. In H.R. Fox–Bowne, *The Life and Times of John Locke*. Darmstadt: Scientia Verlag Aalen, 2, 377–91.

Locke, J. 1957 [1689]: *An Essay Concerning Human Understanding*. Oxford: Clarendon Press.

Locke, J. (ed. J. Axtell) 1968: *The Educational Writings of John Locke*. Cambridge: Cambridge University Press.

Locke, J. 1988 [1689]: *Two Treatises of Government*. Cambridge: Cambridge University Press.

Lukes, S. 1974: *Power: a radical view*. London: Macmillan.

Madison, J., Hamilton, A. and Jay, J. 1987 [1788]: *The Federalist Papers*. Harmondsworth: Penguin.

Mann, M. 1986: *The Sources of Social Power*, Vol. 1, *A History of Power from the Beginning to AD 1760*. Cambridge: Cambridge University Press.

Marcuse, H. 1955: *Eros and Civilization*. Boston, Mass.: Beacon Press.

Marcuse, H. 1972: *One Dimensional Man*. London: Abacus.

Marshall, T. 1950: *Citizenship and Social Class*. Cambridge: Cambridge University Press.

McCarthy, T. 1992: The critique of impure reason: Foucault and the Frankfurt School. In T. Wartenberg (ed.), *Rethinking Power*. Albany: State University of New York Press, 121–48.

Miller, P. 1987: *Domination and Power*. London: Routledge.

Miller, P. and Rose, N. (eds.) 1986: *The Power of Psychiatry*. Cambridge: Polity.

Mills, C. W. 1959: *The Power Elite*. New York: Oxford University Press.

Nietzsche, F. 1967: *On the Genealogy of Morals*. New York: Random House.

Nozick, R. 1974: *Anarchy, State and Utopia*. Oxford: Blackwell.

Oestreich, G. 1982: *Neo-stoicism and the Early Modern State*. Cambridge: Cambridge University Press.

Oldfield, A. 1990: *Citizenship and Community: civic republicanism and the modern world*. London: Routledge.

Parsons, T. 1969a: On the concept of political power. In idem, *Politics and Social Structure*. New York: Free Press, 352–404.

Parsons, T. 1969b: The distribution of power in American Society. In idem, *Politics and Social Structure*. New York: Free Press, 185–203.

Pasquino, P. 1992: Political theory of war and peace: Foucault and the history of modern political theory. *Economy and Society*, 21 (1), 77–89.

Pateman, C. 1988: *The Sexual Contract*. Cambridge: Polity.

Patton, P. 1989: Taylor and Foucault on power and freedom. *Political Studies*, 37 (2), 160–76.

Patton, P. 1993: Politics and the concept of power in Hobbes and Nietzsche. In P. Patton (ed.), *Nietzsche, Feminism and Political Theory*. London and New York: Routledge, 144–61.

Patton, P. 1994: Foucault's subject of power. *Political Theory Newsletter*, 6 (1), 60–71.

Pocock, J. G. A. 1975: *The Machiavellian Moment: Florentine political theory and the Atlantic republican tradition*. Princeton: Princeton University Press.

Rabinow, P. 1989: *French Modern: norms and forms of the social environment*. Cambridge, Mass.: MIT Press.

Raeff, M. 1983: *The Well-Ordered Police State: social and institutional change through law in the Germanies and Russia, 1699–1800*. New Haven and London: Yale University Press.

Rawls, J. 1972: *A Theory of Justice*. Oxford: Oxford University Press.

Rose, N. 1990: *Governing the Soul: the shaping of the private self*. London: Routledge.

Rose, N. and Miller, P. 1992: Political power beyond the state: problematics of government. *British Journal of Sociology*, 43 (2), 173–205.

Rousseau, J.-J. 1968: *The Social Contract*. Harmondsworth: Penguin.

Sandel, M. 1982: *Liberalism and the Limits of Justice*. Cambridge: Cambridge University Press.

Skinner, Q. 1984: The idea of negative liberty. In R. Rorty, J. B. Schneewind, and Q. Skinner (eds.), *Philosophy in History*. Cambridge: Cambridge University Press, 193–221.

Skinner, Q. 1990: The republican idea of political liberty. In G. Bock, Q. Skinner and M. Viroli (eds.), *Machiavelli and Republicanism*. Cambridge: Cambridge University Press, 293–309.

Small, A.W. 1962: *The Cameralists; the pioneers of German social policy*. New York: Burt Franklin.

Smith, A. (ed. R. H. Campbell and A. S. Skinner) 1976: *An Inquiry into the Nature and Causes of the Wealth of Nations*. Oxford: Clarendon Press.

Smith, A. (ed. R.L. Meek et al.) 1978: *Lectures on Jurisprudence*. Oxford: Clarendon Press.

Taylor, C. 1986: Foucault on freedom and truth. In D. Hoy (ed.), *Foucault: a critical reader*. Oxford: Blackwell, 69–102.

Taylor, C. 1989: Taylor and Foucault on power and freedom: a reply. *Political Studies*, 37 (2), 177–83.

Tully, J. 1989: Governing conduct. In E. Leites (ed.), *Conscience and Casuistry in Early Modern Europe*. Cambridge: Cambridge University Press, 12–71.

Turner, B. S. 1986: *Citizenship and Capitalism: the debate over reformism*. London: Allen and Unwin.

Ullman, W. 1965: *A History of Political Thought: the middle ages*. Harmondsworth: Penguin.

Ullman, W. 1966: *The Individual and Society in the Middle Ages*. Baltimore: Johns Hopkins University Press.

von Neumann, J. and Morgenstern, O. 1944: *The Theory of Games and Economic Behaviour*. Princeton: Princeton University Press.

Wartenberg, T. E. 1990: *The Forms of Power: from domination to transformation*. Philadelphia: Temple University Press.

Wartenberg, T. E. (ed.) 1992: *Rethinking Power*. Albany: State University of New York Press.

Weber, M. 1978: *Economy and Society: an outline of interpretive sociology*. Berkeley: University of California Press.

Wrong, D. 1979: *Power: its forms, bases and uses*. Oxford: Blackwell.

Index

absolute power
  Locke 48–9
agents 9, 25, 115, 132,
  147–9, 157
citizens 72
classes 83
Giddens 9, 23–4
rational 73, 76
see also consent,
  subjects
Arendt 10–11
Aristotle
  on citizens 102
art of government
  Foucault 110–12
authorization
  Hobbes 15, 36–9, 42, 47,
    55
  Locke 60
autonomy 131
  Habermas 91–2
  individuals 94–7, 104,
    149–50
  Marcuse 89–90

moral agents 21, 96, 132,
  147–50, 157

Bachrach and Baratz 4
bureaucracy
  Foucault 135
  Weber 135

Christianity 121–2
citizens 4, 20, 41, 57, 70–2,
  81, 83–4, 93, 99, 109,
  117, 119, 133–4
  Aristotle 102
  consent 132–3
  Dahl 66
  liberty 42
  Locke 59
  republican 43, 73–4
  see also agents, consent,
    government, legitimacy,
    subjects
civil law 17, 58–9, 61
civil society 18, 64, 73,
  80–6, 89, 93, 95

Lightning Source UK Ltd.
Milton Keynes UK
UKOW051903021111

181375UK00001B/9/A